CONSUMER'S GUIDE TO

FEEDING BIRDS

*What Bird Owners Need to Know
About What's Good—and What's Not—
for Their Pets, and Why*

LIZ PALIKA

HOWELL
BOOK
HOUSE

New York

Howell Book House

A Simon & Schuster/Macmillan Company
1633 Broadway
New York, NY 10019

Library of Congress Cataloging-in-Publication Data

Palika, Liz, 1954–
    The consumer's guide to feeding birds: What bird owners need to know about what's good—and what's not—for their pets, and why / Liz Palika.
        p.   cm.
    Includes bibliographical references and index.
    ISBN 0-87605-641-9
        1. Cage birds—Feeding and feeds.   2. Cage birds—Nutrition.
3. Consumer education.   I. Title.
SF461.75.P35   1997
636.6'8—dc21   97-1167
                                              CIP

Manufactured in the United States of America
10 9 8 7 6 5 4 3 2 1

CONTENTS

DIRECTORY OF CHARTS

INTRODUCTION

The idea for this book and its companion books *(The Consumer's Guide to Dog Food, The Consumer's Guide to Cat Food* and *The Consumer's Guide to Feeding Reptiles)* grew out of my efforts to find the "perfect" foods for my pets. My husband and I have always shared our home with a number of different pets, usually dogs, cats, birds and reptiles of assorted sizes and shapes.

Because some of our pets have had special needs, I wanted to find out what's in pet foods. What are all those ingredients? What is *by-product meal?* Or even stranger, what is *digest?* Why are there so many different ingredients? And why are there so many different vitamin and mineral supplements? If the food is as good as the advertisements say, why do we need all those supplements?

I became so intrigued by the subject of nutrition that I re-enrolled in college and am now doing postgraduate studies in nutrition. I've found it to be a fascinating area of study!

I have also come to a few conclusions. First, food does make a difference. I have found that my pets' good health is directly related to good nutrition. Second, there is no one food that is right for every pet; even pets of the same species. Each bird, cat, dog or tortoise has its own specific nutritional needs.

I also have found—sometimes to my dismay—that researchers, nutritionists and other experts disagree, sometimes vehemently. One researcher might state one fact—with research to back him up—while another researcher will argue exactly the opposite, and he will also have studies to back his opinion!

Since there are still plenty of points on which the experts disagree, we are all left with choices to make. This book was written to give you, the bird owner, the knowledge and tools to make those choices when you feed your bird. I cannot tell you what food to feed your bird. However, I can give you the tools to make your own decisions.

As you are trying to find the right food for your bird, if you have questions about your bird's health please consult an avian veterinarian.

This book was read by an experienced avian veterinarian before its publication; however, it was not written to replace good veterinary care.

Liz Palika

and my very willing bird food taste test participants: Pretty Bird, a cocka-tiel; Bingo, an African Grey; Gonzo, a cockatoo; Ma and Pa, two very prolific zebra finches; and Hansel and Gretel, two happy budgies.

ONE

BIRDS AS PETS AND BIRD FOODS

Birds have been kept as pets for as long as we have recorded history. Legend says that around 750 B.C., Romulus and Remus, the founders of Rome, were suckled by a she-wolf and fed by a woodpecker (why a woodpecker?). In medieval times, during the bubonic plague, songbirds were kept in sickrooms supposedly to absorb the foul vapors. Thousands of canaries have accompanied miners underground to give notice of deadly fumes. Hawks and other birds of prey have hunted with and for their royal owners for thousands of years.

In more recent history, birds have maintained a celebrated place in the United States. George Washington had a green parrot who could sing, and Thomas Jefferson had a tame mockingbird. Ulysses S. Grant had a Mexican parrot, and Calvin Coolidge's wife kept canaries in the White House.

Songbirds have enthralled and entertained people for generations, bringing a bit of color and song into a sometimes dreary life. Parrots and other birds that can learn to talk have been taught almost every human language known, including the colorful phrases used by sailors spending long stretches of time at sea.

Why are we so fascinated by birds? Many say it is jealousy because we cannot fly. Other bird owners are intrigued by the varieties of colors and patterns or the musical abilities of birds. Compare the brilliant colors of a scarlet macaw, a goldfinch, a red lory or even the pastels of a cockatiel. Listen to the musical chirping of finches, the songs of a canary or even the harshness of a macaw who thinks he's being ignored. The varieties are tremendous; there is, literally, a bird for anyone who wishes to keep one.

TAKING CARE OF WHAT WE'VE GOT

Although birds have been kept as pets throughout history, it is only recently that we have been concerned about good husbandry and care. For centuries, a bird would be captured, kept in a cage until it died, and then replaced. Very little was known of the birds' needs and rarely were birds bred in captivity.

However, in this century, and most notably the past 20 years, people have become more aware that the supply of animals in the wild is finite. With many species extinct, endangered or threatened, and more natural bird habitats being destroyed, more research is being done to satisfy the needs of birds in captivity. When a bird owner can properly care for a particular parrot, finch or canary, that animal has a better chance to live a longer, healthier life and perhaps even reproduce.

Captive bird breeding has grown tremendously in the past 20 years, again because research has shown that supplying the proper environment, conditions and nutrition for a particular animal can eliminate some of the stress of captivity and make it possible for the birds to reproduce. Captive breeding has enabled more people to own birds as pets by producing those birds in a safe, healthy environment.

Birds caught in the wild are always stressed by their capture and the change in their environment, some more than others. They may also be loaded with parasites or suffer from injuries or disease. However, when raised by a knowledgeable breeder, captive-bred birds are normally healthy, parasite-free and well adapted to their captive environment.

Today, humans are still the greatest danger to wild birds, but overall life for many species is looking up. More and more people each year are owning captive-bred birds as pets and treasuring them as companions. Veterinary care is also improving, and knowledge about birds' needs is increasing. Bird owners are learning how to care for their birds properly. New products arrive in stores regularly—products that allow bird owners to provide a better, safer environment for their birds. And our knowledge of nutrition is improving, too, so that bird owners can feed their pets better.

BIRD FOODS

For as long as birds have existed, they have foraged or hunted for themselves. Some birds eat seeds, others eat fruits, some eat insects and some sip nectar. Some birds eat reptiles, some hunt for fish and others are opportunists that eat just about anything. Instinctively, each species follows certain guidelines as to what it should eat.

However, captivity changed that. A bird that normally forages for certain seeds may be fed different seeds or even pelleted food. Can a bird that is genetically programmed to forage for unripe and ripe grass and weed seeds eat a pelleted food made from foreign (to the bird) ingredients? How will the bird's system adjust to that? Will there be nutritional problems later? Are some of the behavior problems seen in captive birds related to nutritional problems? Why do some birds kept in captivity look different from their wild cousins? These are just some of the issues facing avian researchers as pet bird ownership increases, along with the demand—and need—for answers. Many of the researchers work for commercial bird food manufacturers, trying to develop products that supply avian nutritional needs. But are they succeeding?

ABOUT COMMERCIAL PET FOODS

The first known commercial pet foods were prepared in England from the carcasses of horses that died in harness on London streets. Butchers would sell the leftovers—entrails, brains and other scraps—packaged especially for pet food.

In the United States, in 1926 the Purina Company established the Pet Care Center for testing new animal foods. The first Purina dog food, Dog Chow Checkers, received rave reviews from Admiral Richard Byrd, who used it to feed his sled dogs in Antarctica. Since Purina already had a reputation for producing good food for domestic animals, especially swine and poultry, dog owners were willing to give the new food a try.

After World War II the idea of pre-prepared pet foods really caught on. These foods were a convenience, just like drive-through restaurants and frozen dinners, and those conveniences were much sought after by American women after the war.

Most of the early pet foods were for dogs and cats and were meat-based, usually beef or horse meat. Although grains and other non-meat sources of nutrition were available to pet food manufacturers, these ingredients were not often used because researchers didn't believe dogs or cats had the digestive enzymes to break down the crude fiber or cellulose present in grains, beans, seeds and many vegetables.

However, things changed again in 1956 when a research team working for Purina developed a controllable cooking process called extrusion. Extrusion cooking enabled feed grains to be used in pet foods for the first time, and by the mid-1970s prepackaged pet foods had become a big business. Today pet foods are a multi-billion dollar industry and, in fact, in many grocery stores pet foods cover more aisle space than baby foods.

Prepackaged bird foods began appearing in pet stores in stages. Some of the early foods were simply bags of seeds, usually millet and/or sunflower seeds. Sometimes pelleted foods made for other species (such as monkeys, bears or other omnivores) were re-packaged and sold as food for larger birds. However, the late 1980s and early 1990s saw a great increase in the number of different prepackaged birds foods available for many types of birds.

Why so many foods? The bird owner may buy the food, but the primary consumer is the bird. A food that is not eagerly eaten will certainly not benefit the bird in any way. Of course, some birds will eat anything that is placed in front of them, but many more are discriminating about what they eat. Bird owners are certain to notice when the bird is not eating or is not eating with its normal enthusiasm.

Bird owners want to feed their pet a food that is nutritionally balanced, affordable and relatively easy to feed. Bird owners will go to incredible lengths to provide food for their pets, including chopping vegetables, cutting up fruit or buying insects. However, if easier, healthy alternatives are available, many bird owners welcome them eagerly.

Most bird food companies have spent time and money researching and developing new foods with four goals in mind:

1. To meet the needs of the bird's owner.
2. To make a food the bird will eat.
3. To meet the bird's nutritional needs.
4. To make a profit.

To meet all four of these goals, developing a bird food usually takes years. Many factors come into play: What is the purpose or goal of this food? Is it going to target a specific population, such as finches? Canaries? Conures? Parrots? Or is the target population more general, such as all seed-eating birds? What are the proposed ingredients? Are those ingredients readily available? What do those ingredients cost? Who is the target buyer of the food?

When a recipe is proposed for a bird food, the ingredients are then analyzed. What is the nutritional value of each ingredient and how do these ingredients work together? Will they meet or surpass the nutritional needs of the birds being fed?

Other factors in the recipe must also be researched. In what order should the ingredients be added? How long should the food be cooked and at what temperature?

As test batches of the food are produced, they are sent back to the laboratory and further analyzed before final testing. If the food passes these tests, it is produced in limited quantities and fed to birds to test palatability (taste). A food does the bird absolutely no good unless it is eaten. Palatability tests determine whether or not a number of different birds will eagerly eat the food. Because a new food may attract (or, depending upon the bird, repel) simply because it is new or different, the tests are repeated for several days or even weeks to make sure the food has staying power.

If a new food makes it this far, it is then fed to a number of birds for a period of time, and detailed records are kept as to the birds' health and well-being. Most bird food manufacturers maintain populations of birds to eat (and therefore test) their foods. Birds are monitored for growth, color and appearance, appetite and overall health. Food acceptance is also important.

Control studies are often done, comparing similar birds fed a known diet to the same species of birds fed the new diet. Researchers measure body weight, growth, blood profiles, skin and feather condition, color and general health.

Some food manufacturers ask breeders, veterinarians, zoos or other bird owners to test new foods. A bird breeder or veterinarian may feed a certain number of birds the new food while feeding other birds their normal diet. By comparing a number of different factors, including overall health, color and appearance, and breeding success, the food manufacturer can evaluate the food.

Even with such rigorous testing, you, as the wise consumer, must keep in mind that pet foods are big business; these pet food companies are in business to make a profit. Each company's goal is to get you to buy its food. As a wise consumer, you must be knowledgeable enough to choose the bird food (or foods) that will best suit your pet. Read on!

TWO

UNDERSTANDING NUTRITION

Throughout history, food in its various forms has been used as medicine. My grandmother seemed to think chicken soup could cure just about any illness. Almost all human cultures have a number of foods—not just herbs, but everyday foods—that are recommended for all kinds of circumstances. Over the years, these old wives' tales have been replaced by modern medicine. Modern medicine developed certain "magic bullets"—aspirin, antibiotics and so on—and in the process forgot many of the ancient wisdoms by which humanity has survived for thousands of years.

THE PRICE OF PROCESSED FOODS

These magic bullets have indeed increased longevity and cured many diseases, but at what price? People and their domestic animals are suffering from malnutrition at alarmingly higher rates, and many researchers believe our overly processed foods are to blame. We are, literally, cooking the nutrients out of our foods.

Other researchers are recognizing more food allergies than were previously known, both in people and in animals, and believe this, too, is due to our reliance on processed foods. Obesity has also become a major health hazard, for people and even for our birds.

We have forgotten many of the lessons those "old wives" taught us about foods and herbs and how to use them to create and maintain good health, relying instead on magic bullets to cure all our problems. However, in more recent years researchers, nutritionists and alternative medicine practitioners have found that many of those old remedies do, in fact, have medicinal properties, and these properties should be part of good daily nutrition.

This attitude toward food emphasizes its importance, because without food we would die. With a poor diet, one that does not meet our nutritional needs, we may live, but we will not live as long or as well. With a good diet that does satisfy our nutritional needs, our odds of living better are drastically increased. The same applies to birds.

GOOD FOOD EQUALS GOOD HEALTH

It is vital that you have an understanding of good nutrition and how it affects your bird's health. Good nutrition is needed for a strong immune system, reproduction and normal growth. Foods supply the needed substances that regulate the body's many processes, including organ development and functions. Food is necessary to resist disease, for healing, and as a source of energy so that the bird can function and live from day to day.

Nutrition is the relationship between food and the health of the body. The body—in this case, your bird's—takes in food and, through chemical changes, digests it.

Birds come in several different "eating" forms. Some birds eat mice, fish or other live prey while others eat only seeds or other plant material. Some birds eat fruit and nectar while others eat anything they find in front of them. This variety makes feeding birds a challenge. Specific foods or diets must be formulated for each species to meet their individual nutritional needs.

THE DIGESTIVE PROCESS

It would be impossible to thoroughly explain bird digestion in these few short paragraphs because of the incredible variety of birds and their required diets. However, it is necessary that you, as the bird owner, understand a few basics about digestion so that you have a better understanding of nutrition.

All of the foods eaten by the bird must be broken down by the body into simpler chemical forms. This process is called digestion. With birds, digestion starts in the crop. The crop is a pouch located at the base of the esophagus that stores food for a short period of time. Food passes from the crop to the stomach, which is made up of two parts. The proventriculus, or the glandular part of the stomach, secretes digestive juices that help break down foods. Food then passes to the ventriculus, or the gizzard, a very muscular part of the stomach where the food is ground up with the help of grit, gravel, sand or pebbles the bird has swallowed. The amount or size of the grinding material depends upon the size of the bird and the bird's normal diet. The type of bird makes a difference, too, as some birds produce more digestive enzymes than others.

As the food (which is already mixed with digestive juices) passes from the stomach into the intestinal tract, some of the food is broken down into simpler chemical forms and is absorbed into the body. Depending upon the nutrient, some of the food is absorbed into the bloodstream through tiny blood vessels in the small intestine. Other nutrients are channeled through the lymph system. During this part of digestion, water-soluble vitamins are picked up by the bloodstream.

The liver also plays an important part in the digestive process by changing some of the nutrients into products needed by the individual cells. Other nutrients are stored by the liver for future use.

"The process of metabolism involves all of the chemical changes that nutrients undergo from the time they are absorbed until they become part of the body or are excreted from the body," Lavon J. Dunne wrote in the *Nutrition Almanac: Third Edition*. Those chemical changes are incredibly complex. The body is constantly working with these nutrients, constructing body chemicals such as blood, enzymes and hormones, or breaking down compounds to supply the cells with energy.

THE IMPORTANCE OF LIGHT

Researchers specializing in human medicine discovered that many people suffer from a seasonal disorder that causes them to get depressed, moody and lethargic in the winter. These people are adversely affected by the shorter daylight hours, less sun and increased cloud cover. When they are exposed to lights of a specific type, however, the effects of this disorder can be greatly reduced.

Light is just as important to birds. Ultraviolet light helps birds build up body cholesterol and convert it to vitamin D3. This vitamin is necessary for the proper absorption of calcium.

Natural periods of light and dark are also important. Never leave a light on for 24 hours; instead, a natural photoperiod of 12 on and 12 off is preferred. If you decide to breed your animals, you may need to adjust the photoperiod even more to mimic natural daylight hours.

Birds instinctively know they need light and tend to perch in bright places. A full-spectrum light, such as those sold for reptiles, will satisfy your bird's needs.

Zoo Med offers a fluorescent light called Repti Iguana Light UVB 310 that is designed specifically for iguanas. Zoo Med claims this light produces the complete ultraviolet spectrum present in sunlight in the tropics at noon. Many keepers of tropical birds have used it with good results. Zoo Med products are available at many pet supply stores.

National Biological Corporation also produces a fluorescent light that is supposed to produce the needed rays. They claim their Reptile D-Light duplicates natural sunlight with a full 8 percent UVB concentration. You can call the company at (800) 891-5218.

The feces excreted by the bird are body wastes, that is, normal waste material produced by the bird's body plus undigested food material. When researchers study the digestibility of a particular food, the feces are analyzed. The formula, stated very simply, is the amount of nutrients ingested, minus the amount of nutrients in the feces, equals the apparent digestibility of the food.

Birds have very short digestive tracts, even relative to their small size. To compensate, "The bird's digestive system is extremely efficient. Fruit eaters will digest and eliminate berries within thirty minutes, and seed and nut eaters will digest their food in only three hours," according to Sheldon L. Gerstenfeld, DVM, author of *The Bird Care Book.*

ALL ABOUT FEATHERS

Why do birds have feathers? Most people would say prehistoric birds developed feathers so they could fly. Fossil evidence, however, suggests that early birds developed feathers millions of years before they developed flight. Originally, it seems that feathers appeared simply to provide warmth.

Today, feathers provide warmth, protect wild birds from the elements and from skin injuries, allow birds to fly and provide an amazing variety and combination of colors.

There are three main types of feathers: contour, down and filoplume. Contour feathers form the main plumage of the wings, tail and body. These feathers give the bird its shape (or contour), streamlining it for flight and, often, waterproofing it. If you look closely at a contour feather, you can see it is made up of a number of interlocking parallel barbs. If you run your fingers against the grain of this feather, you can disconnect the barbs, thus destroying the integrity of the feather.

Down feathers form the plumage on nestlings and on adults, and are found under the contour feathers. Down insulates the bird from the weather. Down feathers have a short shaft and the barbs do not interlock.

Filoplume feathers are hair-like feathers with a thin stalk and a few soft barbs near the tip. They are associated with contour feathers and may be sensory or decorative.

Birds molt each year to replace old, worn out or damaged feathers. Some birds, including many parrots, will lose and replace feathers year-round. Other birds will molt after breeding season, once the young are raised and weaned. Still other birds depend upon the change of seasons to stimulate the molt. Molting is natural and should not be cause for alarm unless it is prolonged or the bird starts picking at itself or scratching or plucking the new feathers. During a molt, the bird will need a diet slightly higher in protein (feathers are made of keratin, a fibrous protein also found in human hair).

Feather color is the result of pigment and/or structure. Buffs, red browns, dark browns and blacks are caused by melanins, which are pigments synthesized by the bird. Yellows, oranges and reds come from cartenoid or lipochrome pigments that originate, at least in part, in the food the bird eats. Blue colors come from a feather's structure—a thin, porous layer of keratin lies over melanin pigment. Most greens result from the addition of yellow pigment to the structural blue color. Iridescent colors are formed when the thinly laminated structure of the feather barbules is enhanced by underlying melanin deposits.

Why do birds come in so many different colors? Some of the colors enable the birds to blend in with their background and evade predators. But what about the brilliantly colored birds? In many species, the drabber-colored female looks for a brighter-colored male to breed with. One theory is that the brightest male has to be stronger and wilier to survive because he doesn't blend into the background. And because he has survived to breeding age with this handicap, it makes him a better partner. If a female breeds with him, her offspring may be better equipped to survive, too.

Where do those bright colors come from? Heredity is one source, obviously. The brighter-colored male will pass his genes on to his off-spring and chances are they will be brighter in color, too. Bird breeders have been using this concept for years, especially with canaries. There are now many different types and colors of canaries that were never seen in the wild. These selectively bred birds may have different postures, body shapes, colors, spots and singing voices.

Although it is a widely debated subject, many researchers believe that beta carotene also plays a part in feather color. Some say birds fed a diet high in beta carotene, either naturally from foods (grated carrots, grated yellow squash, dark greens) or from a supplement, will be more brilliantly colored than birds not fed this diet.

Many reptile breeders and keepers agree with this theory, and are feeding their herbivorous reptiles beta carotene (or foods high in beta carotene) in an effort to make their reptiles' skin colors more brilliant.

Reptile researchers have long known that many species of reptiles can survive and breed in captivity but do not achieve the coloring often seen in their wild cousins. Is diet a part of this? Only more research will tell us, and in the process that research may answer some of the questions bird breeders and keepers are asking about their birds.

FACTORS AFFECTING GOOD NUTRITION

Proper nutrition means all of the body's essential nutrients are being supplied by the food that is being eaten, in a form the bird's body can use. Those needs include appropriate amounts of protein, fat, carbohydrates, vitamins, minerals and, of course, water.

Each individual bird, of every species, will have slightly different needs for good nutrition. Things that affect nutrition include:

- the type of bird
- the bird's age
- state of general health

- whether or not it is being used in a breeding program
- its activity level
- stress levels
- the food the bird is normally eating

TYPE OF BIRD. As mentioned earlier, each type of bird has certain nutritional needs. Some need meat, some need fish, some need fruits, pollens and greens, some need nectar, some need fruits and nuts. The variety is endless, and it all must be taken into account when formulating a diet for your bird.

AGE. Nutritional needs vary dramatically with the bird's age. Young, active, rapidly growing birds often require more food, more calories or even significantly higher protein levels than do adult birds.

GENERAL HEALTH. Nutritional needs can vary dramatically depending upon the bird's health. A bird stressed by injury or disease will need more support from a good food to meet the increased needs of its immune system and for healing. A bird that is carrying a heavy load of parasites will need medical attention to fight off the parasites and will need nutritional support to regain good health. Good nutrition can also help prevent many health problems by helping to keep the immune system running properly.

REPRODUCTION. Good nutrition is necessary for both the male and female, both before and during breeding. The male that is not well nourished may not produce viable sperm and may even have a reduced desire to breed. If the female is not well nourished, she may not ovulate properly, may not release eggs or may not have the reserves herself to adequately nourish the eggs. It's important that she be healthy before breeding and that her nutritional needs are being met.

ACTIVITY LEVEL. Some birds are, by nature, less active than others. Birds that are more active need nutritional support from their food to maintain their activity level.

STRESS LEVEL. Stress can be many things to a bird. It could be a change in its cage, a change in the location of its cage, a change in cage companions or a change in owners or caretakers. Stress can come from the environment, too, including high noise levels, improper lighting, incorrect humidity and more.

Although good nutrition can help some animals deal better with stress, birds are notorious for their sensitivity to some stresses that no amount of good food can overcome.

FOOD. The food your bird is eating can cause stress, too, especially if the food is of poor quality, is made up of ingredients that are not easily digestible or is simply not the right food for your bird. Too much or too little food can be a problem, too, for obvious reasons.

FOOD AND THE BODY

There is no single thing that can ensure good health. Good health is a jigsaw puzzle with many pieces to it. For most birds, good health requires good food of the proper kind, correct lighting, the right temperature range, the proper humidity and a secure cage of the right size and type. An environment relatively free of physical dangers, excess chemicals and insecticides will also help maintain your bird's good health. And of course, attention from you, the bird's caretaker, is important as well.

Proper nutrition is vital for maintaining the immune system. Your bird's immune system is a marvel, even to researchers who spend their careers studying it. The immune system is an army that fights viruses, bacteria and disease. Every breath brings with it potentially deadly warriors, ready to strike, as does the dirt in the backyard or the water sitting out in an open dish. Unless you soak it in bleach, the sponge you use to clean your bird's cage is probably covered with bacteria that could, without a healthy immune system, cause untold trouble.

An immune system can be weakened by inadequate nutrition, and this could lead to a variety of disorders or make existing disorders more serious. On the other hand, a strong immune system, backed up by a healthy diet, can fight existing diseases and can work with the medical treatments prescribed by your bird's veterinarian. Food and good nutrition are vital to the good health of your pet.

ANOREXIA

Many pet owners have been traumatized by their pet bird's unwillingness to eat, and unfortunately, there is no easy answer to the problem. Birds stop eating for a number of different reasons.

Disease and/or parasites can cause anorexia. Improper husbandry practices, especially regarding temperature and humidity, are common problems. A chilled bird may huddle on a perch without eating. Changes in the environment, including new family members, a new bird or other pet, strange noises, even a new cage, can all trigger changes in the bird's eating habits. Fumes from cooking, from construction, street paving or other sources may cause anxiety and anorexia.

When a bird refuses to eat, veterinary intervention is needed. Birds have a very fast metabolism and must eat often. Don't wait until the bird is weak and starved; that is much too late, and the bird may never recover.

CANCER AND FOOD

Cancer is a word that strikes terror into the hearts of many people. There is much that researchers know about cancer, but much, much more that is not known. We know that cancer cells can grow very rapidly, can create their own blood supply and can invade local tissues. Using very simplistic definitions, these abnormal growths are called tumors. Those that are relatively harmless are said to be *benign*; those that spread and damage surrounding tissues are said to be *malignant.*

Many researchers believe every living body (human, bird and otherwise) has some cancer cells. Normally, the body's immune system reacts to these cells and either destroys them, inhibits their spread or in some other (as yet unknown) manner prevents them from forming tumors. Cancer results when the immune system, for whatever reason, fails to react to the forming tumor cells.

Dr. Gregory Ogilivie of Colorado State University College of Veterinary Medicine and Biomedical Sciences studied dogs with lymphoma and found that cancer changes the way a dog uses or metabolizes nutrients. In a three-year study, dogs treated for lymphoma with conventional chemotherapy were fed a special diet. The diet didn't cure the lymphoma, but it did extend life for anywhere between nine months to a year. Studies have shown similar results for people, and although we do not yet know if birds would have the same reaction, many researchers believe this is very possible.

Unfortunately, there are no known foods that will cure cancer, and the only prevention is to make sure the bird is eating a nutritious diet that will keep the immune system strong and healthy. Amazon parrots have a tendency to develop cancer when they are older.

CONSTIPATION AND BLOCKAGES

It's important for the bird owner to know the normal elimination habits of each particular bird and keep track of eliminations. Although constipation is not common in birds, a blockage or severe constipation can kill a bird in a relatively short period of time.

A blockage or constipation can be caused by the bird ingesting too much gravel or grit, or too large a piece of gravel. It can also be caused by a tumor or a retained egg.

When the owner is familiar with the bird's normal habits, a change is easy to spot and prompt attention can sometimes prevent disaster. A few drops of mineral oil will sometimes help the bird pass the blockage; however, if this isn't successful, contact your veterinarian as soon as possible.

DIARRHEA

A change in diet can sometimes cause diarrhea. If you switch a seed-eating bird over to pelleted food too quickly, it may develop diarrhea. Too much fruit for a bird not accustomed to fruit may set it off. However, diarrhea is often a sign that the bird is suffering from internal parasites of some kind or is hosting some protozoa, bacteria or other disease-causing organisms. Again, see your avian veterinarian before the bird becomes dehydrated.

FEATHER PICKING

Feather picking (or plucking) can be caused by many things, including viral diseases, giardia (a protozoa), bacterial diseases or even fungal infections. However, malnutrition or an inappropriate diet can cause feather picking, too. Because there are so many potential causes, veterinary care is needed to help find the underlying cause of the problem.

GASTROINTESTINAL DISORDERS

Gastrointestinal disorders can be caused by a variety of problems, including parasites, infections, metabolic imbalances, tumors and injuries. It is also amazing what some birds will eat, especially if they are allowed some freedom. Birds will sample silk plants, play with and sometimes eat coins, string, brightly colored plastic, even rocks.

Some gastrointestinal disorders can be caused by the food the bird eats. Feeding a poor quality food, an inappropriate food or a spoiled food can cause gastrointestinal upset or will show up later when the bird is suffering from malnutrition. Gastrointestinal disease may cause symptoms such as poor stools, poor feather growth or even baldness.

JOINT DISORDERS OR LAMENESS

A lame bird is, potentially, a seriously ill bird. A bird with a sore leg or foot will have difficulty perching and, therefore, difficulty eating. To compound the problem, sometimes poor nutrition causes lameness.

Sore feet can be the result of dirty perches, all the perches being the same size (causing cramping) or overgrown nails. Lameness can also be caused by a sprain or other injury.

Young, rapidly growing birds that do not get enough protein, calcium, phosphorus and vitamin D3 may develop bone abnormalities. Thick joints, decreased appetite and problems moving may point to a nutritional problem. Veterinary care is needed right away.

OBESITY

Obesity is one of the newest problems in birds. Rarely are birds in the wild obese. However, birds who find food placed in front of them regularly will, naturally, eat the food, and in the process use no calories finding or hunting the food.

Overweight birds are more prone to a variety of health problems, depending upon the species. Because this is such a relatively new problem to birds, the full extent of the dangers are only now being discovered.

POISONS

Birds are very sensitive to environmental poisons. If your bird has free run of your house, or of one room, make sure your house plants are all nontoxic. Be careful spraying for fleas or other insect pests; those sprays may kill your bird, too. Fumes from Teflon pans may sicken your bird, as may fumes from spray paint, craft projects or glues.

Other poisons may be commonly found around your home. Don't feed your insect-eating bird insects from your yard if you or any of your neighbors put out snail bait or spray for insects. Don't pick rose or other flower blossoms for your bird if you routinely spray with fungicides or insecticides.

Read labels on all household and garden products before using them, and if you are in doubt, call your avian veterinarian or call the company that makes the product.

THYROID

Hyperthyroidism is the overproduction of hormones by the thyroid gland. Symptoms may include nervousness, fatigue, weight loss and rapid pulse. Hypothyroidism is the underproduction of hormones and results in decreased appetite, dull, dry skin, clumsiness, lack of vigor and, in breeding males, lowered sperm count.

Although both types of thyroid disease can be inherited, nutrition can also play a role. Many foods contain soybeans and soybean meal, both of which are incomplete protein sources, lacking several essential amino acids. If other ingredients don't make up for this amino acid loss, the bird may lack tyrosine, the amino acid that stimulates the thyroid gland to produce more hormones. Although studies investigating this relationship are continuing, birds with thyroid disease or a genetic predisposition to it should not be fed commercial foods high in soy.

LONGEVITY

Although many things contribute to how long a bird will live, including its species, heredity, environment and general health, several studies have linked good nutrition to longevity. A diet that supplies the bird's nutritional needs is vital to good health, which, in turn, goes hand in hand with long life.

THREE

THE BASIC BUILDING
BLOCKS OF FOOD

There are eight basic building blocks of nutrition present in the food your bird eats. They are:

- water
- enzymes
- protein
- carbohydrates
- fats
- fiber
- vitamins
- minerals

These nutrients contain chemical substances that affect the body in various ways. They might provide the body with energy or assist in the regulation of body processes, or they might provide for the growth and repair of tissues.

Each of these nutrient building blocks has its own purpose, its own function, but it does not work alone. All of the nutrients are required, in different amounts, for a well-balanced diet. The amounts a bird needs may vary, depending upon the bird and factors such as age, general health, activity level and environment (as discussed in Chapter Two).

In this chapter we will discuss six of the eight basic building blocks:

- water
- enzymes
- protein
- carbohydrates
- fats
- fiber

In Chapter Four we will continue with vitamins and minerals.

WATER: THE MAGIC LIQUID

A simple substance, water is one of the most abundant and important resources of our planet and one that is taken for granted more than anything else. However, without water life as we know it would cease to exist.

The body of most types of birds is approximately two-thirds water. Blood is slightly over 80 percent water, muscles are over 70 percent water and the brain is almost 75 percent water. Even bones are 20 percent water.

Water is required for the normal functioning of every cell in the body. Respiration, digestion, metabolism and elimination all require water. Water is needed to dissolve and transport nutrients. Water keeps all things in balance; only oxygen is more necessary to preserve life.

A certain amount of water is lost each day through respiration and elimination and must be replaced. The amount of water each bird needs can vary depending upon the species involved, the bird's size, its activity level and the climate, especially the temperature and humidity.

Water needs can also vary depending upon the natural climate of the bird. Many desert-dwelling birds have been genetically programmed to conserve water and may get much of their needed water from the food they eat. Many desert birds also know how to sip drops of condensed water off of plants. Tropical birds, however, are genetically programmed to live in a humid, water-rich environment. Many of these birds relish a daily shower or a light misting from a spray bottle.

To make sure your bird's water needs are met, all birds should have clean, fresh drinking water available at all times.

ENZYMES: THE ESSENTIAL BUILDING BLOCKS

Enzymes have numerous essential functions in the bird's body—so many, in fact, that a bird couldn't live without them. Enzymes are made up of two parts: one part is the protein molecule and the other is called the coenzyme. This coenzyme may be a vitamin or a chemical derivative of a vitamin. Enzymes work by initiating a chemical reaction so that other substances can do their job.

Digesting and metabolizing food requires a complex system of enzymes to make sure that thousands of different chemical reactions happen as they should. In the digestive processes, each enzyme is capable of breaking down one specific substance. For example, an enzyme designed to break down carbohydrates does not metabolize fats, and the enzyme that breaks down milk products does not break down carbohydrates. (Breaking down the food means changing the nutrients so they become available for use by the body.)

Because enzymes are made up of proteins and other substances, usually vitamins, the number of enzymes available for use by a bird can vary and can depend upon the bird's diet.

PROTEIN: THE FOUNDATION FOOD

Next to water, protein is the most plentiful element in an animal's body, representing approximately 50 percent of each cell in the body. Proteins are incredibly diverse, serving as building blocks of feathers, nails, skin, muscles, tendons, cartilage and other connective tissues. Protein is one of the most important food elements for growth, development and repair of body tissues, sexual development and metabolism. Proteins are also vital parts of the bloodstream, the immune system, the digestive system, hormone production and much, much more.

AMINO ACIDS. During digestion, amino acids are formed when large protein molecules are broken down by chemical action into smaller molecules. Amino acids are interesting molecules; they are both the end process of protein digestion and the molecules from which protein can be constructed.

Amino acids are vital for the transmission of nerve impulses, and as a result are needed for muscular contractions and for conducting electrical impulses in the brain and spinal cord. Amino acids are involved in the formation of DNA and in the functioning of the immune system. The body's chemistry is so interwoven and so dependent upon other substances and chemicals that an imbalance of even one amino acid can throw the whole system out of kilter.

Protein sources that contain all of the amino acids, such as lean meat or whole eggs, are called complete proteins. Sources of protein that do not contain all of the amino acids, such as soybeans, wheat and corn, are called incomplete proteins.

GETTING THE AMOUNT RIGHT. Besides being a major building block in your bird's body, protein can also be used as a source of energy. When carbohydrates are not available for use by the body in times of need, proteins can be metabolized in their place. In addition, excess protein that is not needed for body functioning or repair can be converted into fat by the liver and stored for future use.

Since excess protein is stored as fat, too much protein can be detrimental to your bird's health. It can also have other potentially serious results, including possible kidney failure. Therefore, excess protein is not advised—more is definitely *not* better in this situation.

Protein deficiencies may result in growth abnormalities, especially skeletal deformities. The skin may also be affected, depending upon the extent of the deficiency. Protein deficiency may also show up as a lack of energy and stamina, mental dullness and even depression. With protein deficiency, there will also be a noted weakness of the immune system and the bird will become open to infection and disease.

SOURCES OF PROTEIN. The bird that consumes live foods (such as insects) will obtain some of the protein it needs from those foods. Birds eating seeds get varying amounts of protein. Millet is about 13 percent protein, sunflower seeds about 15 percent and flax seed about 24 percent protein.

Commercial pelleted bird foods vary, but they usually supply between 14 and 16 percent protein. The protein is from a number of different sources; some, as discussed above, are complete proteins, containing all of the essential amino acids, while others are not. Along the same lines, some of the protein sources are more digestible by the bird than others. For these and other reasons (including cost to the manufacturer and availability), most bird foods have more than one source of protein.

Commercial bird foods commonly have eggs as a protein source. Meat by-products (meat and bone meal, liver, organ meats and other meat products) are protein sources, too, although they are less commonly found in bird food.

Many different vegetable proteins are also commonly used, including wheat in various forms (whole wheat, wheat germ, wheat flour), corn, rice, soy, barley and other grains. Some bird foods will include alfalfa meal, carrots, peas, beans or potatoes.

CARBOHYDRATES: THE ENERGY BUILDING BLOCKS

Carbohydrates are the major element in most plants, accounting for 60 to 75 percent of the dry matter weight of plants. Like proteins, carbohydrates have more than one function in a bird's body.

Carbohydrates supply energy for bodily functions and are needed to assist in the digestion of other foods. Carbohydrates also help regulate protein use and are one of the most important sources of energy for muscular exertion.

Most of the carbohydrates present in foods come in the form of sugars, starches or cellulose.

Sugars and starches are easily digested and are converted into a simple sugar, such as glucose. The body uses glucose as fuel for the muscles, the brain and the nervous system. Excess glucose (sugar from plant material) is converted to glycogen and is stored in the liver and the muscles for future use.

Cellulose is not easily digestible by birds, but it serves as fiber, which we'll discuss a bit later.

SOURCES OF CARBOHYDRATES. Vegetables and grains that supply proteins to the bird can also be a good source of carbohydrates. Corn, rice, oats, potatoes and wheat are easily digested after processing and are good sources of carbohydrates, too.

FATS: NECESSARY BUILDING BLOCKS

Dietary fats, called lipids, are a group of compounds that are not soluble in water and have a number of different functions in the bird's body. Some lipids are a part of cell structures, others are a part of the blood plasma. Lipids also serve as carriers for the fat-soluble vitamins—A, D, E and K.

Fats are also involved in many different chemical processes in the body. And fatty layers under the skin serve as insulation against heat loss. In addition, fats are a source of energy. They furnish more than twice the number of calories (or energy) per gram than carbohydrates or protein.

An important component of lipids are the fatty acids. The alpha-linolenate acids are three fatty acids (oleic, linoleic and linolenic) that cannot be manufactured by the bird's body and must be supplied by food. These acids are necessary for normal growth; healthy blood, arteries and nerves; normal kidney function and healthy, supple skin.

As with many other dietary needs, different birds have different fat requirements. Too much fat can lead to obesity and its associated problems. A fat deficiency in a young animal will initially show up as slow growth. A rare fatty acid deficiency may show up as liver disease, pancreatitis or chronic digestive disorders.

SOURCES OF FATS. Commercial bird foods generally have fat of some kind, usually animal fat, as one of their ingredients, with the amount of added fat based upon the needs of the animal for which the food was formulated. Usually the percentage of fat in a commercial pelleted food ranges from 4 to 8 percent. Seed-eating birds get plenty of fat from their seed when fed a balanced seed mixture. Millet has a fat content of about 4 percent; sunflower seeds are about 30 percent fat and niger seeds can have a fat content as high as 40 percent. It is rarely a good idea to add additional fat to the diet of any bird, with the exception of aviary (outside) birds exposed to severe winter weather. Then, additional fat in the form of suet can be a healthy addition to the diet.

FIBER: THE "ACTION" BUILDING BLOCK

Fiber is the part of food that the bird's body does not digest. The cellulose in fruits and vegetables is one example. Just because it is not digested doesn't mean it's worthless or wasted food, though. Fiber is necessary for good intestinal health because it absorbs water and aids in the formation and movement of feces.

BALANCING NUTRIENTS

All of these nutrients work together, as do the other building blocks we'll look at in the next chapter. Each bird species has its own dietary needs for protein, fat, carbohydrates and fiber, as well as the other nutrient building blocks, and we'll examine those needs in more detail in upcoming chapters.

CHART 1
NUTRITIONAL COMPARISONS OF COMMON BIRD SEEDS

	%Moisture	%Protein	%Fat	%Carbohydrates	%Fiber	%Calcium	%Phosphorus	%Ash
Canary grass seed	7	14	4	56	12	0.05	0.55	6
Flax seed	7	25	37	20	6	0.25	0.60	4
Hulled oats	10	12	4	65	13	0.1	0.35	4
Millet, common	9	14	4	60	10	0.04	0.4	4
Millet, spray	13	15	6	60	11	0.03	0.33	6
Milo	13	12	4	70	3	0.03	0.30	2
Niger seed	7	20	44	13	12	0.44	0.60	4
Safflower	8	15	28	17	32	—	—	3
Sunflower	7	15	28	18	30	0.2	0.5	3

FOUR

THE OTHER BUILDING BLOCKS: VITAMINS AND MINERALS

The discovery of vitamins in 1910 was one of the most exciting achievements in the field of nutrition. Before their discovery, researchers knew that certain substances were needed for good health but didn't know what those substances were. Although nutritionists and researchers have learned much about vitamins since their discovery, experts readily admit there is still much that is unknown, including how much of many vitamins is needed for good health.

For example, in 1970 Linus Pauling created havoc in the nutritional and medical fields when his experiments showed that massive doses of vitamin C could prevent or cure many diseases in people. Research is still continuing, both for people and for our animals, and that research is constantly producing therapeutic applications for vitamins.

WHAT ARE VITAMINS AND WHAT DO THEY DO?

Vitamins are organic substances found only in plants or animals. With a few exceptions, a bird's body cannot synthesize vitamins; therefore, vitamins must be supplied in food or in supplements.

In your bird's body, vitamins work together and with enzymes in a variety of important functions, including:

- digestion
- metabolism
- growth
- reproduction
- cellular reproduction
- oxidation

Vitamins are required for tens of thousands of different chemical actions. Because vitamins work on a cellular level, a vitamin toxicity or deficiency can have a number of different, potentially lethal repercussions. Plus, the levels required for toxicity or deficiency can vary among types of birds, making it even harder to decide what your bird should eat or which problems are nutrition related.

SHOULD YOU SUPPLEMENT?

Deciding which vitamins your bird should get and in what quantities is very difficult, even for researchers. Some researchers believe a diet of natural foods contains adequate amounts of vitamins and minerals, and that over-supplementation can destroy the nutritional balance of the food and even be hazardous to the animal's health.

Other researchers believe a certain amount of supplementation is needed for several reasons, the most important being that a captive diet is not a natural diet. A seed-eating bird in the wild is not eating a diet comprised mostly of millet; it is eating a variety of things, including many different types of seeds, ripe seeds as well as green seeds, plant matter and probably a few insects, too. Even nectar-eating birds do not just eat nectar. In the wild these birds will eat nectar, pollen, insects and probably some plant matter.

Before you decide whether or not to add a vitamin supplement to your bird's food, there is a lot more you need to know. First, you need to understand vitamins and minerals and how they affect your bird's health. Then in the following chapters, we'll discuss what birds eat, natural foods, live foods, commercial foods and their quality, and supplements themselves. Plus, you need to remember that one supplement is not good for every bird.

MAINTAINING A BALANCE

When discussing your bird's vitamin and mineral needs, it's important to keep in mind that no one vitamin or mineral functions alone; each has its own function and place in the system but each is also dependent upon the others. Even if you or your veterinarian decide your bird has a deficiency, you must remember to keep the balance of all the nutrients when you supplement your pet's diet.

INDIVIDUAL VITAMINS EXPLAINED

VITAMIN A. Vitamin A is a fat-soluble vitamin that has two forms: carotene and vitamin A. Carotene, which is found in plants, must be converted into vitamin A before it can be used by the body. Pre-formed vitamin A is the result of that chemical conversion and is found in animal tissues. As a fat-soluble vitamin, excess vitamin A is stored in the liver, in fat tissues, lungs, kidneys and the retinas of the eyes.

Vitamin A is an important antioxidant that helps in the growth and repair of body tissues, aids in digestion and protects mucus membranes, aiding in disease resistance. A substance that enhances the immune system, vitamin A is also necessary for building strong bones, good feathers and claws, and healthy blood. Vitamin A is also responsible for good eyesight.

A vitamin A deficiency will cause slow or retarded growth, reproductive failure and skin disorders. Secondary infections are also common, as are eye disorders.

Because vitamin A is a fat-soluble vitamin, too much can be toxic. (Excess amounts of water-soluble vitamins are excreted in the urine, but extra fat, along with the vitamins it contains, is stored in the body.) Too much vitamin A has also been associated with bone deformities, joint pain and bleeding.

Vitamin A can be found in green leafy vegetables such as spinach and broccoli, and in yellow and orange vegetables such as carrots and squash. Yellow corn, rape seed and millet also contain usable quantities of vitamin A. It is also found in fish oils and animal livers.

Most commercial bird food and supplement manufacturers add vitamin A in one form or another to their commercial food or supplement, rather than depending on the bird food ingredients to retain the vitamin during processing.

THE B VITAMINS. There are a variety of B vitamins. This group is often called the vitamin B complex and includes B1 (thiamine), B2 (riboflavin), B3 (niacin), B5 (pantothenic acid), B6 (pyridoxine), B12 (cyanocobalamin) and B15 (pangamic acid). The B complex also includes biotin, choline, folic acid, inositol and para-aminobenzoic acid (PABA).

The B complex vitamins help provide energy by assisting in the conversion of carbohydrates to glucose, which is the body's fuel. The

B vitamins also help metabolize protein and fat. These vitamins are needed for normal functioning of the nervous system, for good muscle tone and for healthy skin.

Vitamin B1 (thiamine) works with enzymes to help convert glucose to energy. Also known as the "morale" vitamin, thiamine works with the nervous system and is beneficial to a good mental attitude. Although B1 is known to improve individual learning capacity in children and is suspected to work the same way for birds and other animals, this has not yet been proven in birds.

Vitamin B2 (riboflavin) assists in the chemical breakdown of foods. It also works with enzymes to help cells make use of oxygen. Riboflavin is also needed for good vision, healthy skin and nails.

Vitamin B3 (niacin) works with enzymes to metabolize food. It is also effective in improving circulation and reducing cholesterol, and is important in maintaining a healthy nervous system.

Vitamin B5 (pantothenic acid) stimulates the adrenal glands, which increases production of adrenal hormones necessary for good health. Vitamin B5 aids digestion, is good for healthy skin and also helps the body better withstand stress.

Vitamin B6 (pyridoxine) is necessary for absorption of vitamin B12. It also helps linoleic acids function better in the bird's body. B6 is needed for the production of red blood cells and antibodies.

Vitamin B12 (cyanocobalamin) contains cobalt, which works with enzymes to assist in normal DNA synthesis. B12 also works with the nervous system and the systems that regulate appetite and food metabolism.

Vitamin B15 (pangamic acid) works to eliminate hypoxia (oxygen insufficiency) in body tissues, especially muscles. B15 also stimulates the glandular systems.

The other B complex vitamins also serve vital functions:

Biotin assists in the oxidation of fatty acids and in the metabolism of other foods. Biotin is also required by the other B vitamins for metabolism. A deficiency of biotin can cause an abnormal molt.

Choline functions with inositol as a basic ingredient of lecithin, a nutrient important in cell structure and metabolism. A deficiency of choline, combined with a shortage of manganese, can cause a disease called perosis, or fatty liver.

Folic acid works with vitamins B12 and C to metabolize proteins. Folic acid is also necessary for the formation of red blood cells.

All of these B vitamins are water soluble and as a result, excess vitamins are excreted instead of being stored in the body. Because the vitamins are not retained, they must be replenished in the diet. The B complex vitamins can be found in brewer's yeast and whole grain cereals.

Sulfa drugs and insecticides can destroy these vitamins in the digestive tract.

It is also important to remember that most of the B vitamins work together; if they are given as a supplement, they should be given together. An excess of one B vitamin could cause a deficiency (or excess) of another.

VITAMIN C. Vitamin C has caused more uproar than any other vitamin available. In humans, vitamin C has been labeled a "miracle" vitamin because of its ability to fight the common cold. Vitamin C also fights bacterial infections, maintains collagen, helps to heal wounds and prevents some hemorrhaging. And it helps in the formation of red bloods cells. Perhaps most important, vitamin C is known to help boost the immune system, fighting and killing viruses.

However, even though vitamin C has so many beneficial properties, many researchers do not believe birds need vitamin C supplements. Most birds are able to synthesize vitamin C internally, and these researchers believe any additional vitamin C would be wasted. Some researchers also think excess vitamin C can cause a change in the pH balance in the kidneys.

However, many other researchers believe otherwise. Alfred Plechner, DVM, stated in his book, *Pet Allergies: Remedies for an Epidemic,* "I do believe in vitamin C. It can indeed be helpful in many ways for many animals. Among other things, vitamin C contributes directly to adrenal health and function." Other experts think vitamin C can help prevent orthopedic problems in fast-growing young birds.

As the debate continues, many bird food manufacturers are adding vitamin C to their foods, sometimes using ascorbic acid as a preservative. Granted, the amount used to preserve food is small, has a short shelf life and is usually mixed with other substances; however, it is a vitamin C supplement.

At this point, research (and debate) is ongoing, and until some definitive answers are found it will be up to the individual bird owner whether or not to supplement vitamin C.

VITAMIN D. Known as the sunshine vitamin, vitamin D can be acquired from food or can be absorbed during exposure to the sun. There are three forms of this vitamin: D1, D2 and D3. Mammals use D1 and D2, but birds use D3.

Vitamin D is needed for normal calcium-phosphorus metabolism by facilitating the absorption of calcium in the intestinal tract and the assimilation of phosphorus. Vitamin D is needed for normal growth, healthy bones and eggs.

Vitamin D works in conjunction with vitamin A, and a deficiency of vitamins A or D can lead to rickets and other bone diseases and deformities. It can also lead to vision problems and kidney disease.

Vitamin D is a fat-soluble vitamin, and excess is stored in the liver, brain and skin. Too much vitamin D can lead to excess calcium and phosphorus in the system, causing calcification in the blood vessels, soft tissues and kidneys.

VITAMIN E. Vitamin E, a fat-soluble vitamin, is actually a group of substances called tocopherols. Found in cold-pressed vegetable oils, raw seeds, nuts and soybeans, tocopherols are antioxidants—substances that oppose oxidation in the bird's body. Fat oxidation results in free radicals that can cause extensive damage to the bird's body by inhibiting proper bodily functioning. Vitamin E protects both the pituitary and adrenal hormones from oxidation, as does the vitamin B complex and vitamin C.

Vitamin E is important for reproduction. It also assists in the cellular respiration of muscle tissue, including the heart. Vitamin E dilates the blood vessels, allowing more blood to reach the heart, and it works to prevent blood clots from forming in blood vessels.

Many bird food manufacturers add vitamin E to their foods, often using tocopherols as preservatives along with ascorbic acids.

VITAMIN K. Vitamin K is necessary for blood clotting and for normal liver functions. A fat soluble vitamin, toxicity and abnormal blood clotting can result from too high a dosage. The best sources of vitamin K are green leafy vegetables, eggs and fish oils.

CHART 2
SOURCES OF VITAMINS

Vitamin	Common Sources*
Vitamin A	Dairy products, leafy green vegetables, fish liver oil, carrots
Vitamin B complex	Brewer's yeast, whole grain cereals, liver
Vitamin C	Fruits and vegetables, especially broccoli, cabbage, leafy green vegetables
Vitamin D	Sunshine, dairy products, fish liver oil
Vitamin E	Cold-pressed vegetable oil, meats, raw nuts and seeds, leafy green vegetables, soybeans
Vitamin K	Kelp, alfalfa, yogurt, egg yolks, fish liver oil

*Note: These sources are listed not just for direct feeding, but also as sources of the nutrients present in prepared commercial foods.

CHART 3
VITAMIN DEFICIENCIES AND EXCESSES

Vitamin A

Deficiency: Vision problems including blindness and other eye diseases; deficiency disease in Amazon parrots; slow growth; skin problems; diarrhea; abscesses in the mouth, throat or nasal passages.

Excess: Nausea; vomiting; diarrhea; bone deformities; bleeding disorders; dry, flaky skin; skin lesions.

Vitamin B Complex

Deficiency: Fatigue; irritability; nervousness; muscle tremors; convulsions; anorexia; skin problems.

Excess: Water soluble; when taken as a complex, the excess is usually excreted in the urine. An unusual excess can cause nerve damage, blood or digestive disorders.

Vitamin C (Research is ongoing and much debated)

Deficiency: Shortness of breath; swollen joints; slow healing; poor immune system response; skin ruptures or cracks.

Excess: Water soluble; most excess is excreted in the urine. High doses can result in diarrhea.

Vitamin D3

Deficiency: Rickets; bone deformities; poorly developed muscles; nervous disorders; vision problems; metabolic bone disease.

Excess: Increased frequency of urination; nausea; vomiting; muscular weakness; calcification of muscles and organs, including the heart and the kidneys; renal failure.

Vitamin E

Deficiency: Blood and bleeding disorders; collagen problems; breakdown in amino acids; reduced functioning of several hormones; reproductive failure; muscle tremors; muscular dystrophy.

Excess: Generally considered nontoxic; however, it can cause elevated blood pressure.

Vitamin K

Deficiency: Bleeding disorders; reproductive failure.

Excess: Unknown, but generally considered nontoxic.

ALL ABOUT MINERALS

Minerals are present, to some extent, in the tissues of all living things. They make up parts of your bird's bones, beak, muscles, blood and nerves. Minerals help keep the bones strong and the nerves healthy and reactive.

Minerals work with vitamins, with enzymes and with each other. For example, calcium and phosphorus are so closely related and their functions are so intertwined, they could actually be called one mineral: calcium-phosphorus. But they are really two minerals that function best together. Many other vitamins and minerals work the same way. The B complex vitamins also need phosphorus for best metabolism; iron needs vitamin C for best absorption; and zinc helps vitamin A to be released from the liver. A deficiency in any one mineral can have drastic effects on many systems in the body.

INDIVIDUAL MINERALS, EXPLAINED

CALCIUM AND PHOSPHORUS. As was just mentioned, calcium and phosphorus are two separate minerals, but their functions are so closely intertwined that they could almost be referred to as one combined mineral. Calcium is needed for muscle contraction and neuromuscular transmission and for blood coagulation. Calcium is also vital to some of the body's enzyme reactions.

Because it is present in every cell, phosphorus plays a part in almost every chemical reaction in the body. It is part of the digestion process, and in the production of energy it helps stimulate muscle contractions, including the heart muscle. Phosphorus is also a vital part of cell reproduction.

Working together, the most important function of calcium and phosphorus is to strengthen bones. However, too much phosphorus will inhibit calcium metabolism, resulting in calcium deficiencies.

A calcium deficiency can cause rickets, bone, eggshell and skeletal disorders, and malformations. Moderate deficiencies may cause muscular cramps, joint pain, slow pulse and impaired growth. Calcium-phosphorus imbalances are, unfortunately, quite common in rapidly growing young birds.

Many commercial bird foods have among their ingredients bone meal or calcium carbonate, either of which is a good source of these nutrients. For many birds the easiest way to supply calcium is to hang a cuttlefish bone in the bird's cage. However, a cuttlefish bone is calcium and to be used in the body, it must be supplemented with phosphorus from elsewhere in the diet. (See Chart 4 for some sources of dietary phosphorus.)

CHLORIDE. Chloride is found throughout the body and helps regulate the correct balance of acid and alkali in the blood. Working with salts, chloride maintains pressure in the cells that enables fluids to pass in and out of cell membranes. It is also needed by the liver to filter wastes from the system.

A deficiency is usually rare, as chloride is found in table salt and most diets contain adequate amounts of salt. However, a deficiency of chloride can cause impaired digestion and poor muscular contraction.

COPPER. Copper assists in the absorption of iron, which is required to synthesize red blood cells. Copper is also involved in the healing process and helps oxidize vitamin C. Copper is needed to build strong bones, to synthesize phospholipids and to form elastin (a component of connective tissue).

A copper deficiency results in a type of anemia, much like that caused by an iron deficiency. A deficiency can also cause bone or skeletal abnormalities.

Copper is found in liver and fish, as well as whole grains and legumes. The amount of copper found in plant sources can vary depending upon the richness of the mineral in the soil where they were grown.

IODINE. Iodine is a trace mineral that is vital to the proper functioning of the thyroid gland. It plays an important part in regulating the body's energy, in promoting growth and in stimulating the rate of metabolism.

A deficiency of iodine can cause hypothyroidism (an abnormally low secretion of the thyroid hormones), obesity, sluggishness, nervousness and irritability.

Iodine is found in fish. Although it does not occur naturally in salt, salt often has iodine added. Many commercial bird foods add iodine or potassium iodide as a supplement.

IRON. Iron, working with protein, is present in every living cell in the body. The primary function of iron is to combine with protein and copper to make hemoglobin, which transports oxygen in the bloodstream. Iron also works with enzymes to promote protein metabolism. In addition to proteins and copper, iron needs calcium to work properly.

A deficiency of iron can cause anemia, whose symptoms can include difficulty breathing and constipation.

Mynahs, lories, macaws and other parrots have been known to develop iron storage disease, where the birds are unable to flush excess iron from their bodies. Jim Goetz, president of Marion Zoological Inc., makers of Scenic Bird Foods, explains, "Although the mechanism is not as well understood as we would like, our data suggests that because citrus fruits are low in copper, the ceruloplasmin transport mechanism is impaired. We believe that this copper transport mechanism is essential in the reduction of iron to its blood soluble form."

Iron is found in liver, lean meats and fish. Leafy green vegetables, whole grains and legumes also contain iron.

MAGNESIUM. Magnesium helps promote the absorption and metabolism of vitamins and other minerals, including vitamins C and E, calcium, phosphorus, sodium and potassium. Magnesium is also important to protein and carbohydrate metabolism. It aids bone growth and, in fact, more than 70 percent of all magnesium is located in the bones. A deficiency of magnesium will cause cardiac irregularities, muscle twitches and tremors and depression.

Magnesium can be found in leafy green vegetables, raw wheat germ and other whole grains, soybeans, milk, fish and oil-rich nuts and seeds. It is important to keep in mind that cooking, especially at high temperatures, removes magnesium from food. The exception is food processed at very high temperatures that is burned and creates ash, of which magnesium is a component.

ZINC. Zinc is a trace element with a number of important functions. It is vital for the metabolism of a number of vitamins, including the B complex vitamins. Zinc is also a part of many different enzymes necessary for digestion and metabolism. Zinc is needed for the healing processes.

Too much calcium in the diet can hamper the absorption of zinc, as can a diet too high in cellulose. A deficiency will show up as delayed sexual maturity, slow or retarded growth or diabetes.

OTHER MINERALS. Several other minerals are important to your bird's good health. Selenium works with an enzyme and vitamin E to protect cells. Selenium is found in both meats and cereals and a deficiency is rare. Manganese, too, works with enzymes and is important to bone growth and reproduction. Cobalt, sulfur and fluorine are other minerals included in your bird's diet.

CHART 4
SOURCES OF MINERALS

Mineral	Common Sources*
Calcium	Meats, bone and bone meal, milk and milk products, nuts, tofu (raw, firm), collard greens, broccoli, beans, grit, gravel and cuttlefish bones
Chloride	Salt (sodium chloride), kelp
Copper	Liver, whole grain products, leafy green vegetables, legumes
Iodine	Fish, kelp
Iron	Liver, oysters, fish, lean meats, leafy green vegetables, whole grains, legumes, molasses
Magnesium	Green vegetables, raw, whole grains, oil-rich seeds and nuts, soybeans, milk
Manganese	Whole grains, eggs, seeds and nuts, green vegetables
Phosphorus	Meat, fish, poultry, eggs, whole grains, seeds and nuts
Potassium	All vegetables, potatoes, bananas, whole grains, sunflower seeds
Selenium	Yeast, organ and muscle meats, fish, whole grains
Sulfur	Eggs, meat, cheese
Zinc	Whole grains, brewer's yeast, wheat germ, pumpkin seeds

*Note: These sources are listed not just for direct feeding, but also as sources of the nutrients present in prepared commercial foods.

CHART 5
MINERAL DEFICIENCIES AND EXCESSES

Calcium-Phosphorus

Deficiency: Rickets; bone deformities; slow growth; irritability; depression; metabolic bone disease; eggshell weaknesses or deformities; reproductive failure.

Excess: Must have a balance between both minerals, according to species.

Chloride

Deficiency: Impaired digestion; poor muscular contractions.
Excess: Adverse reactions suspected but unknown.

Copper

Deficiency: General weakness; impaired respiration; anemia; skeletal abnormalities; skin sores.
Excess: Toxic hepatitis.

Iodine

Deficiency: Enlarged thyroid; dry skin; loss of vigor; slow/poor growth; reproductive failure.
Excess: Unknown.

Iron

Deficiency: Weakness; constipation; anemia.
Excess: Unknown.

Magnesium

Deficiency: Neuromuscular excitability or irritability; tremors; depression.
Excess: Unknown.

Manganese

Deficiency: Slow or retarded growth; reproductive failure; abnormal bone growth; paralysis; ataxia; blindness; deafness.
Excess: Unknown.

Potassium

Deficiency: Respiratory failure; cardiac arrest; nervous disorders; insomnia.
Excess: Unknown.

Selenium
Deficiency: Premature aging; juvenile death; skeletal and cardiac myopathies.

Excess: Hepatitis; nephritis.

Sulfur
Deficiency: Slow or retarded growth; sluggishness; fatigue.

Excess: Unknown.

Zinc
Deficiency: Retarded growth; delayed sexual maturity; diabetes; skin problems.

Excess: Relatively nontoxic, but excessive intake may have harmful side effects.

FIVE

WHAT DO BIRDS EAT?

There is no one diet or food that is right for every bird. Just as birds come in a variety of sizes, shapes and colors, so do their dietary needs. It's important for you, as your bird's owner and caretaker, to provide a diet that satisfies all of your bird's nutritional needs.

How do you know what foods a particular bird might eat? The shape of the bird's beak gives a few clues. Hummingbirds with long, narrow beaks eat (or drink) nectar. Birds with cone-shaped beaks are primarily seed eaters (sparrows, finches, cardinals and pigeons). Birds with long, thin beaks are primarily insect eaters (wrens, warblers, vireos, mockingbirds and titmice). Birds with strong, hooked beaks need them for harder-to-eat foods. Parrots use their strong beaks for fruits and nuts. Hawks and owls need that beak for eating their prey.

Although hawks and falcons have been kept as pets and hunting companions for hundreds of years, they have special requirements that make them difficult for most people to keep. Maintaining these birds requires a great deal of expertise and knowledge of their behavior and nutritional needs. Therefore, most pet birds are either seed eaters or seed, fruit and vegetable eaters. Throughout history, these types of birds have been easier to feed; easier to catch, breed or domesticate; and more pleasing to keep.

As a bird owner and caretaker remember, too, that in the wild a particular species might eat a variety of things. A seed eater might eat seeds, ripe and unripe, from a number of different plants. That same bird might also eat some greens, some insects, some fruit, some pollen or some nectar.

A variety of foods can also satisfy your bird in other ways. As Kathleen Samuelson, editor of *Bird Talk* magazine, has pointed out, "Birds are highly intelligent animals that require physical and mental stimulation. It goes against everything in their being to sit idle in a cage all day long." In the wild, most birds are constantly searching for food. By providing your pet bird with a variety of fun, healthful foods with different textures, tastes and colors, the bird can enjoy some mental and physical stimulation.

BIRD FOODS

GRAINS. Grains include oats, wheat, barley and other grains, including grain products. Many birds will enjoy whole grain breads, pastas, rice and cereals. Grains and grain products are good nutrition when fed in conjunction with other foods and they supply vitamins, minerals, fiber, proteins and carbohydrates.

SEEDS. Many bird owners assume (mistakenly!) that seeds are most birds' natural food and that birds can survive on a diet of only seeds. In fact, a bird eating only seeds will probably suffer from a variety of nutritional health problems because seeds—even a variety of seeds—cannot supply all of the bird's nutritional needs. Seeds lack some vitamins and minerals and can be very high in fat.

Seeds are also only as good as the soil they are grown in. If the soil lacks trace elements or minerals, that deficiency is passed along to the plant and its seeds. In addition, seeds can go bad or "die." If the seeds will not sprout, they are considered dead and less nutritious to the bird. Keep in mind that many birds eat seeds just as they are ripening or even before. The best nutrition is in the growing, ripening seed. Unless it is the dead of winter and the bird is hungry, very few birds will actually hunt for totally ripe, hard seeds.

The most commonly fed seeds include anise, canary grass, flax, hemp, white lettuce, millet (yellow, white and red), milo, niger, oat, poppy, rape, safflower, sesame and sunflower seeds. When feeding seeds, vary the mixture and amounts of seeds, add a vitamin-mineral supplement and feed additional appropriate foods such as grains, vegetables and fruits.

SOME SAFE, NUTRITIOUS PLANTS

Common Name	Form of Plant
alfalfa	fresh; hay; dried; meal; pellets
apple	fresh, no core or seeds
banana	peeled fruit
barley	leaves; hay; meal or flour; sprouted seeds
beans	leaves; stems; sprouts
beets	stems; flowers; grated roots
blackberries	fruit
blueberries	fruit
broccoli	heads; grated stems
brussels sprouts	heads
cactus	de-thorned pads (leaves); blossoms
carrots	root (chopped or grated)
clover	leaves; blossoms; hay
corn	kernels off the cob
dandelion	leaves; stems; flowers
grapes	fruit
grass	fresh; no insecticides or fertilizers
hibiscus	flowers; leaves
kale	leaves
millet	leaves; meal or flour; hay
mustard	leaves; flowers
nasturtium	leaves; stems; flowers
okra	fresh or frozen, thawed; leaves; flowers
parsley	fresh leaves
peas	pods; fruit
pumpkin	fruit
soybean	leaves; hay; meal or flour
spinach	fresh leaves (do not feed to excess)

squash	blossoms; fruit
strawberries	fruit
sunflower	seeds (unsalted); meal or flour
timothy	hay
tomato	fruit *only*
turnip	leaves; grated root
wheat	sprouted seeds; fresh leaves; bran or flour
zucchini	fruit

FRESH VEGETABLES. Vegetables are very nutritious, containing a wide variety of vitamins, minerals and trace elements. In addition, the dark green and orange vegetables are high in vitamin A, and spinach is high in calcium and iron. Some good vegetables to feed most birds include chopped or grated broccoli, carrots (grated for small birds, chopped for bigger birds), collard greens, endive, kale, parsley, squash, sweet potato, tomatoes and zucchini. Fresh sprouts are a good addition to most birds' diets. Some good sprouts are rape, radish, lettuce, mung beans, milo and alfalfa.

FRESH FRUITS. Most birds relish fresh fruit, and for most birds fruit is a good addition to the diet. However, with some special exceptions (such as toucans), fruit should not make up a large portion of most birds' diet. Too much fruit will cause loose stools. Parrots, conures, parakeets and most other seed-eating birds will enjoy a slice of apple, a piece of banana, a slice of cantaloupe, or a strawberry or two. Other good fruits are apricots, grapes, papaya and other berries.

NUTS. Many of the larger hooked-bill birds—such as many of the parrots, macaws and cockatoos—love nuts. Shelled walnuts, almonds and peanuts are good, nutritious foods. Smaller birds accept finely chopped nuts. Many commercial bird foods include nuts (chopped, diced or ground).

MEATS AND INSECTS. As mentioned earlier, many birds that normally eat seeds, nuts and other plant products also eat insects. Even hummingbirds eat insects. Insects can add protein, as well as other nutrients, to the bird's diet. The most common insects to feed to pet birds are mealworms (grain beetle larvae) and crickets, both of which are available from pet supply stores. Many edible insects are also available through the mail. There is a list of some suppliers in Chart 6 at the end of this chapter.

The birds of prey are obviously hunters and meat eaters. Hawks, falcons and owls are proficient hunters. Although these birds are occasionally kept for the sport of falconry, rarely are they kept as pets. Many other birds that are not birds of prey will also eat little bits of meat, especially cooked chicken. Although this sounds somewhat cannibalistic, it is good nutrition. Meat adds protein, calcium and other nutrients to the bird's diet.

However, too much meat can disrupt the bird's digestive bacterial flora, so it should be fed sparingly. Meat should be well-cooked, unseasoned (or very mildly seasoned), and any uneaten food should be removed before it spoils.

GRIT. Seed-eating birds grind their food in a muscular portion of the stomach, called a gizzard, with the help of grit. In the wild birds will occasionally pick up grains of sand or small pieces of gravel and swallow it. The sand or gravel stays in the gizzard and works as a grinding tool to break up hard food. Most researchers suggest placing a bowl of grit, sand or gravel in the bird's cage so the bird can swallow it as needed. Most commercial grit is made up of sand, small pieces of gravel and bits of shell, especially oyster shell.

There is considerable controversy as to which birds need grit and which do not. Some experts recommend that all budgies, cockatiels, lovebirds, parrots, canaries and finches have access to grit. And some experiments have shown that birds with no access to grit eat more food than those that have a supply of grit. Moreover, the health of the bird declines without grit.

As we said, grit is very controversial. However, there is less danger to the bird by giving grit than there seems to be by withholding it. Some birds given larger pieces of grit than is appropriate for their size may suffer a blockage or other injury. A small bowl or feed cup of appropriately sized grit will allow the bird to ingest grit as it is needed.

COMMERCIAL PELLETED FOODS. Commercial pelleted or extruded foods for pets have become commonplace over the last 50 years. There are commercial foods available for dogs, cats, pigs, cattle, goats, horses, monkeys, bears, reptiles and yes, even birds. These foods can either serve as a complete food for your bird or can be used as an addition to

COMMON POISONOUS PLANTS

This is a list of very common poisonous plants, but it is by no means complete. If you have doubts or questions about some plants in your house or yard, call your local hospital's poison control center, your veterinarian or your local nursery.

amaryllis
anemone
apple (seeds only)
avocado (leaves, not
   the fruit)
azalea
belladonna
bird of paradise
bottlebrush
boxwood
buttercup
calla lily
cherry (seeds)
Christmas cactus
common privet
crocus
croton
cyclamen
daffodil
diefenbachia
dogwood
eggplant (foliage)
English ivy
foxglove
hemlock
holly
horse chestnut
hyacinth
impatiens
iris
jasmine

jimson weed
larkspur
lily of the valley
locoweed
marijuana
milkweed
mistletoe
morning glory
mushrooms (some
   wild ones)
oleander
peach (seeds)
pennyroyal
philodendrons
poinsettia
poison ivy
poison oak
poison sumac
pokeweed
potato (foliage)
privet
rhododendron
rhubarb
sage
snapdragon
sweetpea
tomato (foliage)
tulip
verbena
wisteria
yew

EDIBLE INSECTS

Aphids appear in the spring on rose bushes, hibiscus and other shrubs, usually on new growth or flower buds. These tiny green, brown or black insects are too small to nourish many birds but can be a wonderful treat for many baby birds, seed-eating birds, small insect-eating birds or nectar-eating birds. Finches, in particular, relish aphids. You can set a stem of a hibiscus bush complete with aphids in the bird's cage so that the bird can munch as it pleases.

Cockroaches are detested worldwide. These flat-tened, nocturnal insects are great escape artists, and although they seem to be synonymous with dirt and filth, they can infest even the cleanest home. Because of this, very few bird keepers use cockroaches as a food source, even though they are good food. Cockroaches used as food must be free of poisons and baits.

Crickets are found throughout the United States, especially in gardens or areas with good hiding places. Common house crickets are easily cultured domestically and when fed a good diet, are very nutritious. Crickets are best used as a food source for birds after being well fed themselves for a few days—often called *gut loading*. The cricket will then pass that nutrition on to the bird that eats it. You can purchase crickets in pet supply shops, by mail order, or raise them at home.

Earthworms come in many different varieties. Insect-eating birds especially relish a wiggling earthworm. You can dig up earthworms in your backyard (if you don't spray insecticides), or you can cultivate them in a compost heap.

Mealworms is a general term used to describe several kinds of beetle larvae. Some are big, some small, some dark in color, but all are the hard-shelled larvae of beetles. Mealworms (and their beetles) can infest stored grains, and when raised as a bird food they do best when fed grain products. Mealworms, like crickets, are best fed to your bird after gut loading, as the larva will then pass on that extra nutrition.

Slugs are snails without shells, and for that reason are slimy and difficult to pick up. However, they can be good food for birds if you and your immediate neighbors do not put out snail or slug poison. A bird that eats a poisoned slug will most likely die.

Snails are a major garden pest in many areas of the southern United States. Extremely hardy and reproducing rapidly, snails can wipe out a garden in no time. However, snails can also be a good bird treat. Many birds eagerly eat baby snails.

If you live in a part of the country where there are snails, you can supply your bird with a snail snack as long as you and your immediate neighbors do not put out snail poison. If you feed your bird a poisoned snail you risk poisoning your bird, too.

Snails can be found under garden debris, under the edge of a potted plant or in any cool, dark hiding place. Snails are normally out feeding after you have watered the yard or after a rain. Humid evenings will also bring them out.

Sowbugs (*Oniscus asellus* and *Armadillidium vulgare*) are also sometimes called pill bugs, wood lice and armadillo bugs. These bugs are often found under boards, rocks or other yard refuse. They feed on organic material on and in the soil. The compost heap is a great spot for sowbugs.

Many insect-eating and even seed-eating birds will eat sowbugs. Do not feed your bird sow bugs from the backyard if you have recently sprayed with an insecticide or other poison.

your bird's total diet. In Chapter Six we'll discuss commercial foods in more detail.

OTHER FOODS. Birds can eat and enjoy a number of different foods. A bite of scrambled eggs, a spoonful of yogurt or cottage cheese, a bit of toast with peanut butter will both amuse your bird and add to its nutritional good health. As a general rule, if a food is good for you, your bird can probably have a taste of it, too. Just remember to keep snacks and treats to less than 10 percent of your bird's total diet.

WATER. Birds are notorious for soiling their water. Some drop bits of food in the water, or try to bathe in their drinking dish, or relieve themselves in it. All birds should have fresh, clean water in a clean water bowl every day. If your bird is particularly messy, you may need to change the water several times a day.

A drip bottle waterer is fine *if* the bird is using it enough. If not, the danger of dehydration is greater than the danger posed by dirty water. Also, some birds need the humidity that a water bowl can provide.

WHAT DO DIFFERENT BIRDS EAT?

AFRICAN GREYS. African Greys are very intelligent birds; in fact, some experts believe these are the most intelligent birds. Greys learn to talk quite readily and will often talk on their own rather than mimic. They also like to explore their environment, so when unsupervised they must be kept in a strong, secure cage.

Greys eat a varied diet, including seeds, fruits, vegetables and whole grain breads. Greys will eat a commercial pelleted diet readily if started on it when young; however, adult birds can be resistant to change.

These birds eat palm oil seeds in the wild and so need more fat in their diet than most other birds. Sunflower seeds can supply this need.

BUDGERIGARS. Once called parakeets, budgerigars (or budgies) are great little birds. Relatively long lived and hardy, these little birds are bright, animated and cheerful. Budgies will thrive on a varied seed mixture, including canary grass seed, millet, chopped oat groats and broken sunflower seeds. Anise, rape seeds, sesame seeds, flax and milo are also good foods. Budgies enjoy unripe weed seeds, so pick some from your yard or garden (as long as you don't use any pesticides). Some occasional fruits or vegetables will also be welcome.

A mineral block or cuttlefish bone should be available at all times, as should grit.

BULBULS. These beautiful birds will thrive on a variety of fruits, including berries, raisins, currants, bananas, figs, dates and grapes. Bulbuls will also need a good vitamin and mineral supplement and a daily serving of insects of the appropriate size; mealworms are fine.

CANARIES. Canaries are colorful little birds long known for their lovely songs. Only male canaries sing, although the females may chirp quite pleasantly.

Canaries will thrive on a varied seed diet consisting of seeds high in carbohydrates and protein. Canola seeds, rape, oat, niger, hemp and flax seeds are recommended. Canary grass seed, millet, white lettuce seeds and poppy seeds are good. A vitamin and mineral supplement should be sprinkled over the seed. A small piece of apple or banana, or some greens may be offered several times a week. During breeding season, some egg food or egg food treats are good nutrition. A cuttlefish bone should always be available.

Canaries have a very fast metabolism and will eat one fourth of their weight daily. Lack of seed for as little as 24 hours could literally starve a canary.

Carotene can contribute to brighter-colored feathers in canaries, although it will not change what the bird is genetically designed to be. Carotene can be fed naturally from dark green veggies, grated carrots, grated yellow squash, or from a vitamin supplement containing carotene.

COCKATIELS. Cockatiels are one of the most popular pet birds. These gentle, elegant little birds chirp, trill, whistle and sometimes even learn to mimic words. These are active little birds and enjoy toys, treats and attention.

Cockatiels are seed eaters, but seeds alone are not sufficient for good nutrition. Cockatiels also need grain products and will relish rice cakes, popcorn, grain cereal and pasta. Fresh fruits and vegetables such as sweet potatoes, corn, grated carrots, kale, apples and broccoli are good. Many cockatiels will also willingly eat commercial pelleted foods.

COCKATOOS. Cockatoos were one of the first birds kept as pets in Europe and are the most long-lived of the parrots, with a life expectancy comparable to that of humans. They are very intelligent, large birds and need human attention and companionship.

Cockatoos will eat a varied seed mixture with the addition of other foods, including cooked rice and beans, as well as fresh fruits and vegetables. Berries, sprouts and a bit of honey now and then will be welcome. These birds will also eat commercial pelleted foods.

A mineral block in the cage is good for both its content and for beak exercise. However, some experts say grit is not needed for cockatoos, as these birds produce an enzyme that prepares their food for digestion.

Cockatoos like to explore things and play. A millet spray, hard chew treats and colorful toys will help stimulate their minds and alleviate boredom.

CONURES. Conures are medium-size, intelligent birds. They are quick mimics, often learn to talk quite well and can be very loud. Conures do well on a diet of varied seeds, soaked and sprouted seeds, beans, fresh fruits and vegetables. They can usually be easily switched over to a pelleted food.

A mineral block or cuttlefish bone should be supplied and a vitamin supplement fed regularly. Conures in the wild will strip, eat and play with twigs, so a few clean twigs or small sticks now and then will provide fun, some added nutrition, and will help to alleviate cage boredom.

DOVES. There is nothing quite like the soft cooing sounds made by doves. It is so soft, gentle and peaceful. Doves are seed eaters and will thrive on a varied seed mixture consisting of millet, canary grass seed, oats, dehulled cracked sunflower, niger and rape seeds. Hard-boiled eggs, whole grain bread and cooked rice and beans make good treats. A commercial pigeon food is also acceptable.

Doves should have access to clean grit and a cuttlefish bone at all times.

FINCHES. Finches are active, amusing little birds. Like canaries, finches have a very fast metabolism and must have access to fresh, clean food at all times. Most finches will eat approximately one quarter of their weight in food each day.

Finches are seed eaters and will enjoy millet, niger seed, rape seed, hemp and canary seed. Flax seed, anise, oats and poppy seeds are also good. Spray millet is a nutritious treat.

Unripe grass and weed seeds are a part of finches' normal diet in the wild, so if you can provide them, the birds will enjoy it. Finches will also eat finely chopped greens, such as kale, spinach sprouts and broccoli. Grated carrot and a piece of apple are good treats. A special treat might be some dandelion or chickweed.

Finches also need insects, especially when breeding. Small or mini-sized mealworms, chopped mealworms, ant larvae, small cockroaches or other small insects will be eaten eagerly. If no insects are regularly available in their diet, many species of finches will refuse to breed, or if they do breed, will not produce healthy young.

RAISING MEALWORMS

Mealworms, scientifically known as *Tenebrio molitor,* are known pests of stored grains. However, they are also well known as a valuable food source that is readily accepted by captive birds, reptiles and amphibians.

You can buy mealworms in small quantities at pet supply stores or in bulk from suppliers and growers. However, if you feed a number of birds that relish insects and need a quantity of mealworms, they are not difficult to raise.

A five-gallon aquarium with a screen top is a good mealworm enclosure, as the glass sides make it difficult for the worms or beetles to crawl out. Wheat or oat bran makes a good culture medium. Pour about three inches of bran in the five-gallon aquarium. Drop in about 100 mealworms (which you can buy from one of the companies listed in Chart 6 or at your local pet supply store). The mealworms will eat the bran and excrete a sand-like material that will sift to the bottom. Replenish the bran as needed.

In addition, the mealworms will need some moisture. Slice an apple or potato and lay the slices on top of the bran. The mealworms will eat the fruit, leaving the skin, which you can then remove. Do not give the worms open water; it will drown them and cause the bran to mold.

Mealworms have four life stages: egg, larva, pupa and beetle. The mealworm you can buy is in the larva stage. As the larva matures, it will turn into a pupa—looking like something out of a science fiction movie—then into a beetle. Leave the beetles in the culture. They will lay eggs which, in turn, will grow into more mealworms.

Mealworms will grow and move through their life stages rapidly if kept at 75 to 80 degrees. Much less than that and the mealworms will become lethargic and fail to grow.

LORIES. Lories are very intelligent, colorful birds that love to investigate their surroundings. Lories will figure out how to open the latch on their cage door or take toys apart just for the fun of it.

There is much controversy regarding what lories should be fed. Some experts think lories are nectar eaters and should be fed nothing else. Others believe lories can be healthy and hearty eating a wet pelleted food supplemented with sugar water.

"Although nectar may be more natural to lories, a diet of nectar produces very loose, watery, messy stools, making housekeeping chores that much more difficult," according to avicultural expert David Sefton. "Many aviculturists have had success feeding lories pelleted foods. We wean our lories to Pretty Bird pellets."

LOVEBIRDS. Lovebirds are active, playful, colorful, feisty small parrots. Lovebirds, as their name suggests, are devoted mates and parents and usually do better when kept as a pair instead of alone.

Lovebirds are seed eaters and will enjoy fresh fruits and vegetables, as well. Favorites seem to be corn, green beans, apples and grapes. Sprinkle a vitamin-mineral supplement over their food. Lovebirds will also accept commercial pelleted foods.

MACAWS. Macaws are splendid, colorful, large birds that require quite a bit of attention from you. These intelligent birds do not do well alone and need human companionship. Macaws thrive on a varied diet that includes seeds, nuts, a variety of fruits and vegetables, and pelleted food. The seeds and nuts should include sunflower seeds, safflower seeds, canary grass seeds, millet, oat groats, niger seed, peanuts, shelled walnuts and cracked corn.

Macaws like to try new foods, too, and may enjoy sharing your lunch with you. Offer some pasta, legumes or whole grain bread. A hard mineral block should be available for its mineral content and for beak exercise. A vitamin-mineral supplement should also be fed regularly.

MYNAHS. Several different commercial mynah foods are available. However, some experts think some of these foods do not meet the birds' nutritional needs. They recommend supplementing with cooked chicken, cooked beans or legumes. Fresh fruit, peanut butter and dog food may also be fed.

AMAZON PARROTS. Amazon parrots have been popular pets for many years. These charming, intelligent, attractive birds are known clowns; the old adage "anything for a laugh" applies to Amazons. A number of different species belong to the Amazon category of parrots, including the orange-winged, yellow-headed, red-headed and white-fronted, as well as several others.

Amazons need a varied diet that includes seeds, nuts, fresh fruits and vegetables and whole grains. Amazons seem to be prone to obesity in captivity and should be fed seeds lower in fat. Feed limited amounts of sunflower and safflower seeds, and peanuts.

BROTOGERIS PARROTS. These lovely dwarf parrots, also called parakeets (not to be confused with budgies), are great little pets. The Brotogeris include the grey-cheeked parakeet, the white-winged parakeet, the orange-chinned parakeet and the cobalt-winged parakeet, among others.

Brotogeris are seed eaters and require a varied seed mixture as well as a variety of grains, such as whole grain bread. Offer a selection of fresh vegetables and fruits regularly. These little birds will also do well on a commercial pelleted food.

ECLECTUS PARROTS. Eclectus parrots are sweet, calm, sensitive, medium-size birds. Eclectus are seed eaters but relish dark green vegetables for their natural vitamin A content. They also enjoy soft fruits such as apples and bananas, yellow vegetables such as squash and sweet potatoes, and sprouted seeds. Eclectus will also do quite well on commercial pelleted foods.

Pionus Parrots. These tropical parrots are attractive, relatively quiet and very good natured. Pionus includes several different species, including the Maximilian's parrot, the white-cap, the blue head, the dusky-violet and the bronze winged, among others.

Pionus eat seeds, fresh fruits and vegetables. They will also enjoy and thrive on sprouts, cooked beans and legumes, whole grain bread and a millet spray for a treat.

Poicephalus Parrots. Poicephalus, or African parrots, are medium-size parrots that come from different parts of Africa and include the Senegal parrot, the Meyer's, the red-bellied, the brown-headed and the Ruppell's, among others. Compared to other parrot species, these are relatively quiet birds, yet they are still lively and intelligent.

These parrots are seed eaters, thriving on a mixture that includes sunflower seeds, safflower and millet. Fresh fruits and vegetables are also important, including apples, bananas and greens. A cuttlefish bone or mineral block should be available at all times.

Pigeons. Although pigeons have a bad reputation with many city dwellers, they are a species to admire. Pigeons are survivors and live, literally, all over the world. The best known pigeon pets are racing pigeons, or homing pigeons. These birds will race home from incredible distances. A well-trained homing pigeon can return home from as far away as 500 miles, at speeds of up to 50 miles per hour.

Pigeons are seed eaters and prefer the smaller seeds. Many experts, however, recommend feeding commercial pigeon foods rather than a homemade diet because birds that fly long distances have exacting nutritional needs. It's also important to remember that poultry and scratch feeds are not intended for pigeons.

Pigeons should have access to grit at all times. If you feed seeds, add a vitamin-mineral supplement to the pigeon's diet. If you feed a commercial food, supplementation is not needed.

Quail, Pheasants, Partridges and Peafowl. Quail can be kept quite easily by many bird keepers but pheasants, partridges and peafowl can be difficult to keep unless you have adequate room and outside shelter.

All of these birds will eat a varied seed mixture—a finch mix works well—as well as a universal poultry food and a few mealworms (or other insects) daily.

Some sprouts, chopped greens and finely chopped soft fruit (apple or banana) can top off the diet.

STARLINGS. Starlings are often thought to be pest birds, especially by farmers in the Midwest; however, some species make very attractive pets. The splendid glossy starling is from Africa and is an attractive, active bird.

Starlings are omnivores and will readily eat just about anything. Seeds, chopped nuts, various fruits and vegetables, grain products and a vitamin-mineral supplement will nourish a starling quite well.

THRUSHES. The Shama thrush and Dyal thrush have both been kept successfully as pets. These attractive birds have exquisite voices, and are hardy and healthy.

The drawback to keeping thrushes is that they are largely insectivores. You must be able to supply mealworms, earthworms, crickets, white worms and/or maggots. Their diet may be supplemented with hard-boiled then mashed egg, cooked meat, raw ground beef or poultry mash, but the vast majority of their diet must be insects. Grated carrots and finely chopped greens can also supplement this basic diet.

TOUCANS AND TOUCANETTES. These exotic birds should not be kept by a beginning aviculturist, as they do have unique needs. Nutritionally, these birds can eat a commercial mynah bird food supplemented with some additional fresh fruit (papaya, grapes and cantaloupe), peanut butter, soaked dog food kibble and cooked beans and legumes. Toucans should not be fed seeds, nuts or fresh vegetables.

Some experts say that toucans should be fed insects, while others say they can do just fine without. However, in the wild toucans do eat beetles and other insects. Just keep in mind that toucans need protein—either from insects, meats or pelleted foods.

CHART 6
SOURCES OF LIVE FOODS FOR INSECTIVORES*

Company	Phone Number	Products
Arbico	(800) 827-2847	Crickets, waxworms, mealworms, flies
Bassett's	(800) 634-2445	Crickets, mealworms
Drosophila	(800) 545-2303	Fruit flies
Fluker Farms	(800) 735-8537	Crickets, mealworms
Grubco	(800) 222-3563	Mealworms, crickets, fly larvae, waxworms, superworms
Holder	(914) 635-8471	Cockroaches
Manchester Worm Farm	(800) 497-8067	Earthworms, red worms, night-crawlers, earthworm-raising kits
Nature's Way	(800) 318-2611	Mealworms, waxworms, fly larvae, crickets
Rainbow Mealworms	(310) 635-1494	Mealworms, crickets
Ray's Reptiles	(402) 477-1975	Crickets, mealworms, waxworms
Rock Bottom Bait	(904) 463-7760	Mealworms, waxworms, crickets
Testa	(916) 666-0321	Houseflies, fruit flies
Top Hat Cricket	(800) 638-2555	Crickets, mealworms, waxworms

*Note: Some pet supply stores may also sell live insects.

SIX

UNDERSTANDING COMMERCIAL BIRD FOODS AND THEIR LABELS

In previous chapters we discussed your bird's nutritional needs: proteins for energy, to build healthy cells and feathers, and for growth; fats for processing vitamins and healthy skin; carbohydrates and fiber for energy and digestibility; and of course, plenty of clean water. We know that vitamins and minerals often work together and with enzymes for cell function and growth. We even know what foods contain these nutritional building blocks. But how do we know whether or not a commercial food is supplying these needs?

Unfortunately, there is no easy answer. In fact, the nutritional needs of birds and the quality of commercial bird foods are two highly debated subjects—ones that have some researchers fervently defending one position and others arguing exactly the opposite.

"I discovered that many commercial food formulations are woefully deficient in key nutrients," says veterinarian Alfred Plechner in his book *Pet Allergies: Remedies for an Epidemic*. He condemns the quality of the ingredients used by many pet food manufacturers; the moldy grains, rancid foods and the meat meal made from slaughterhouse discards.

However, the pet food companies emphasize the quality of their foods and point to the generations of animals residing in their care centers, eating the food the company produces and looking the picture of health.

In this chapter we'll discuss both sides of the various issues as thoroughly as possible. Ultimately, it's up to you to decide what you want your bird to eat.

DISSECTING THE LABEL

Every bird food label must include specific information, which is usually divided into two parts: the principal display panel and the information panel.

The **principal display panel** is very straightforward. It provides the food's:

1. brand name (Pretty Baby, Wild Birds Unlimited, Kaytee, etc.)
2. identity statement (describes the contents: Finch food formula, Parrot Seed Mixture, etc.)
3. designator (identifies species and growth stage: for hand raising young birds or for adults)
4. quantity of contents (identifies the weight of the contents)

The **information panel** provides the food's:

1. guaranteed analysis (shows the percentages of the food's contents)
2. ingredient list (shows the ingredients, in descending order, by weight)
3. feeding instructions (how much to feed your bird per serving)

The principal display panel is like the name of your town; it identifies where you are but doesn't tell you how to get around. For a "road map" of the food, you need to be able to "read" the stuff on the information panel. Let's review in detail the first two items found on it (the last is pretty much self-explanatory).

GUARANTEED ANALYSIS

The guaranteed analysis on the information panel of the bird food label lists the minimum levels of crude protein and fat and the maximum levels of fiber and water. *Crude* refers to the total protein content, not necessarily the amount of protein that is actually digestible. Therefore, the crude protein and fat amounts are simply rough guides. The actual amount available to your bird depends upon the ingredients and their quality.

The amount of moisture in a food is important, especially when you are comparing foods. A food containing 24 percent protein and 10 percent moisture would have less protein per serving than a food with the same percent of protein listed on the label but only 6 percent moisture. Chart 7 has a conversion formula so you can find the dry matter basis of a food and then discover the actual protein or fat content of that dry matter.

CHART 7
DRY MATTER BASIS CONVERSION

The labels of most bird foods look very much alike until you get to the guaranteed analysis, which looks different. Each food lists protein, fat and fiber levels, as well as moisture levels. To compare the different foods and get a good idea of what the nutritional values really are, you must remove the moisture from the guaranteed analysis and compare the foods as dry matter. For example, consider this analysis:

Brand X Food	**Guaranteed Analysis**
Protein	20%
Fat	10%
Fiber	10%
Moisture	10%

If a food shows that the moisture level is 10 percent, the dry solid matter in the food is 90 percent. To find the protein level of this dry matter, divide the 20 percent protein (from the label) by the 90 percent dry solids. The answer, 22 percent, is the percentage of protein in the actual food.

The guaranteed analysis is only a starting place when reading the label, because it contains so little information. Hill's Pet Products, makers of Science Diet foods, used an advertisement in 1984 that was an excellent demonstration of how the guaranteed analysis on a pet food label could fool the unsuspecting buyer. The ad listed a guaranteed analysis, just like one from a package of bird food, and listed crude protein at 10 percent, fat at 6.5 percent, fiber at 2.4 percent and moisture at 68 percent. Typical numbers for a canned dog or cat food. However, the list of ingredients was a shocker: four pairs of old leather work shoes, one gallon of used crankcase oil, one pail of crushed coal and 68 pounds of water! These ingredients, when analyzed, would equal the guaranteed analysis. Not very nourishing!

INGREDIENT LIST

Ingredients are listed in descending order, by weight. However, the list might be misleading. Suppose canary grass seed is listed as the first ingredient, making you think that it is the primary ingredient. Look again—canary grass seed is followed by wheat flour, wheat germ, wheat middlings and so on. The combined wheat products may well total much more than the canary grass seed. That might be okay if your bird can thrive on wheat, but it could be bad news if your bird needs nutrition other than wheat.

The following is a list of some of the ingredients found in commercial bird foods. These ingredients may or may not be used in bird seed mixtures but they can be, and often are, listed on the labels for pelleted or extruded bird foods. These descriptions are based on the definitions for animal feed established by the Association of American Feed Control Officials (AAFCO).

PLANTS, GRAINS AND OTHER INGREDIENTS

Alfalfa meal is the finely ground product of the alfalfa plant.

Dried whey is the watery part of milk, separated out and then dried. It is not less than 11 percent protein or less than 61 percent lactose.

Barley is at least 80 percent sound barley, no more than 3 percent heat-damaged kernels, 6 percent foreign material, 20 percent other grains or 10 percent wild oats.

Barley flour is the soft, finely ground barley meal obtained from milling barley.

Beet pulp is the dried residue of sugar production from sugar beets.

Ground corn (also called corn meal or corn chop) is the entire corn kernel ground or chopped. It must contain no more than 4 percent foreign material.

Corn gluten meal is the by-product of the manufacture of corn syrup or starch. It is made up of the dried residue after the bran, germ and starch have been removed, and is high-quality protein.

Brewer's rice is small fragments of rice kernels that have been separated from larger kernels of milled rice.

Brown rice is the unpolished rice left over after the kernels have been removed.

Soybean meal is a by-product of the production of soybean oil and is high in protein.

Ground grain sorghum is made by grinding the grains of sorghum.

Cereal food fines is a by-product of breakfast cereal production, consisting of particles of the foods.

Linseed meal is the residue of flaxseed oil production, ground into a meal.

Peanut hulls are the outer hull of the peanut shell, ground.

Dried kelp is dried seaweed. The maximum percentage of salt and minimum percentage of potassium and iodine must be declared.

MEAT OR MEAT-BASED INGREDIENTS

Meat is the clean flesh of slaughtered cattle, swine, sheep or goats. It may be only striated skeletal muscle, tongue, diaphragm, heart or esophagus, overlying fat and the portions of skin, sinew, nerves and blood vessels normally found with that flesh.

Meat by-products are the clean parts of slaughtered animals, not including meat. It does include lungs, spleen, kidneys, brain, liver, blood, bone, partially defatted low temperature fatty tissue, and stomachs and intestines freed of their contents. It does not include hair, horns, teeth or hooves.

Meat meal is rendered meal made from animal tissues. It cannot contain blood, hair, hoof, horn, hide trimmings, manure, stomach or rumen contents, except for amounts that may be unavoidably included during processing. It cannot contain any added extraneous materials or any more than 14 percent indigestible materials; not more than 11 percent of the crude protein in the meal may be indigestible by the bird.

Meat and bone meal is rendered from meat, including bone, but doesn't include blood, hair, hoof, horn, hide trimmings, manure, stomach and rumen contents, except small amounts unavoidably included during processing. It does not include any extraneous materials. No more than 14 percent may be indigestible residue, and no more than 11 percent of the crude protein may be indigestible.

Poultry by-products are clean parts of slaughtered poultry, such as heads, feet and viscera, and must not contain feces or foreign matter except in unavoidable trace amounts.

Poultry by-product meal consists of the ground, rendered, clean parts of slaughtered poultry, such as necks, feet, undeveloped eggs and intestines. It does not contain feathers, except those that are unavoidably included during processing.

Dehydrated eggs are whole dried poultry eggs.

Animal by-product meal is made by rendering animal tissues that don't fit any of the other ingredient categories. It still cannot contain hair, hooves, horn, hide trimmings, manure, stomach or rumen contents, nor any extraneous material.

Animal digest is a powder or liquid made by taking clean, undecomposed animal tissue and breaking it down using chemical and/or enzymatic hydrolysis. It does not contain hair, horn, teeth, hooves or feathers, except in unavoidable trace amounts. Digest names must describe their contents: Chicken digest must be made from chicken, beef from beef, and so on.

Beef tallow is fat derived from beef.

Fish meal is the clean, dried, ground tissue of un-decomposed whole fish or fish cuttings, with or without the oil extracted.

PRESERVATIVES

BHA and BHT are both preservatives. BHA is butylated hydroxyanisole. BHT is butylated hydroxytoluene. According to Dr. Plechner, both have been associated with liver damage, fetal abnormalities and metabolic stress, and have "a questionable relationship to cancer."

Ethoxyquin has been the most highly debated item in commercial pet foods for the last several years. It is a chemical preservative that has been widely used to prevent spoilage in pet foods. Ethoxyquin was approved by the U.S. Food and Drug Administration in 1956, but some researchers have since alleged that it can cause cancer, liver, kidney and thyroid dysfunctions, reproductive failure and more.

An independent testing laboratory is now conducting a new test on ethoxyquin. This test is following testing protocols approved by the FDA. The FDA will evaluate the study before its results are released to the public.

Many pet food manufacturers still use ethoxyquin (see Chart 8). However, because of the public concern, many others have switched to other ways of preserving their foods.

Propionates, calcium propionate and sodium propionate, were recently reevaluated by the FDA and although massive doses of these preservatives did kill lab rats, the FDA labeled them safe. Germany, however, has banned propionates.

Propionic acid is a fatty acid that exists naturally in everything from apples to wood pulp. For bird food manufacturers, it works in two ways: It flavors food and it inhibits mold growth. Recent research shows propionic acid to be a safe preservative.

Sodium nitrate is used both as a food coloring (red) and as a preservative. When used in food, sodium nitrate can produce carcinogenic substances called nitrosamines. Accidental ingestion of sodium nitrate by humans can be fatal. Experts have not said whether sodium nitrates are fatal to birds, but all recommend caution. If a bird food contains sodium nitrates, call the manufacturer and ask for some information on the amounts used and the safety precautions taken regarding birds.

Tocopherols (vitamins C and E) are naturally occurring compounds used as natural preservatives. Tocopherols function as antioxidants, preventing the oxidation of fatty acids, vitamins and some other nutrients. Manufacturers are using tocopherols more frequently as preservatives, as many pet owners are more concerned about chemical preservatives. However, tocopherols have a very short shelf life, especially once the bag of food has been opened.

CHART 8
PRESERVATIVES, ARTIFICIAL COLORS
AND FLAVORINGS

Not all preservatives, artificial colors and flavorings are dangerous or carcinogenic. However, many people are concerned about these additives. The safety of ethoxyquin is still up in the air, for example. This chart points out the contents of some common bird foods and treats. To be sure about what is in your bird's food, read the label carefully and if you have any questions, call the manufacturer.

(If label lists "artificial colors" or "artificial flavorings" but does not specify what exactly is being used, this chart lists it as "not specified.")

Food	Artificial Colors	Artificial Flavorings	Preservatives
8 in 1 Pet Products Ultra-Blend for Cockatiels	red 40, yellow 5, blue 1		potassium sorbate, vitamin E, citric acid
8 in 1 Pet Products Parrot Ultra-Blend Advanced Nutrition Diet for Parrots			BHA, BHT, propyl gallate
8 in 1 Pet Products Iron & Blood Supplement			potassium sorbate
8 in 1 Pet Products Skin & Plumage Food Supplement			propyl paraben, BHT, propyl gallate
Hartz Parakeet High Energy Blend	yellow 5, blue 1	not specified	
Hartz Parakeet Condition Treat	red 40, yellow 5	not specified	
Kaytee Exact Original Hand Feeding Formula			propionic acid, ethoxyquin

Food	Artificial Colors	Artificial Flavorings	Preservatives
Kaytee Exact Rainbow Complete Daily Diet	not specified	not specified	ethoxyquin
Kaytee Exact Original Complete Daily Diet			propionic acid, ethoxyquin
Kaytee Nutra-Puffs Treats	not specified		propionic acid, BHT
Kaytee Molting Conditioning and Color Food for Canaries and Finches			ethoxyquin
Kaytee Gourmet Fruit & Vegetable Treat for Parrots			propionic acid, ethoxyquin
Kaytee Fruit & Vegetable Treat Stick for Cockatiels	not specified		propionic acid, ethoxyquin
Lambert Kay Avimin Mineral Supplement	not specified		potassium sorbate, methylparaben, propylparaben
LM Animal Farms Fruit Cocktail for Finches	not specified	not specified	ethoxyquin
Mardel Laboratories Vita-Flight			BHT, ethoxyquin
Nutriphase Parakeet Formula	not specified		ethoxyquin
Nutriphase Canary Formula	not specified		ethoxyquin

WHAT ARE THOSE OTHER INGREDIENTS?

The National Research Council believes adequate amounts of nutrients can be obtained by eating a well-balanced diet consisting of a selection of the proper ingredients. However, there is much more to nutrition. "Other factors affecting adequate nutrition are insufficient soil nutrient levels, resulting in nutrient deficient foods. Food processing and storage deplete foodstuffs of valuable vitamins and minerals," says Lavon J. Dunne in his book, *Nutrition Almanac.* Many nutrients are also lost or depleted during cooking, especially at high temperatures.

To ensure that their foods are complete and balanced nutritionally, many bird food manufacturers add vitamins and minerals to the food during processing. Sometimes these are added in a natural form, as an ingredient. For example, yeast is added to many foods because it is an excellent source of selenium, chromium, iron, magnesium, manganese and many other needed nutrients.

Natural vitamins and minerals can be separated from their natural source, either plant or animal, and used as additives. The vitamin (or mineral) is considered natural as long as there has been no change to the basic molecular structure.

Vitamins or minerals can also be added to the food in a synthetic, manufactured form. Synthetic vitamins and minerals usually contain a salt such as sulfate, nitrate or chloride, which helps stabilize the nutrient. Most researchers believe the body absorbs synthetic vitamins as well as natural, with very little difference in metabolism. The exception is vitamin E, which works much better in natural form.

Many of the chemicals listed on bird food labels are the chemical names of natural or synthetic vitamins and minerals added to food during processing.

Ascorbic acid is a synthetic form of vitamin C.

Biotin is a natural B complex vitamin.

Calcium carbonate is a natural form of calcium.

Calcium oxide is a natural form of calcium.

Calcium pantothenate is a high potency, synthetic source of vitamin B5.

Calcium phosphate is a calcium salt found in or derived from bones or bone meal.

Chloride or *chlorine* is an essential mineral, usually found in compound form with sodium or potassium.

Choline is a B vitamin found in eggs, liver and soy.

Choline chloride is a high potency, synthetic source of choline.

Cobalt is a trace element, an essential mineral and an integral part of vitamin B12.

Copper is a trace element, an essential mineral that can be toxic in excess.

Copper carbonate is a natural form of copper.

Copper gluconate is a synthetic form of copper.

Copper sulfate is a synthetic source of copper.

Ferrous sulfate is a synthetic, high-potency source of iron.

Folic acid is a B vitamin found in yeast or liver.

Inositol is a B complex vitamin.

Iron oxide is a natural source of iron.

Magnesium oxide is a natural source of magnesium.

Menadione sodium bisulfite complex is a source for vitamin K activity.

Pangamic acid is vitamin B15.

Pantothenic acid is vitamin B5, a coenzyme.

Potassium chloride is a high-potency, synthetic source of potassium.

Potassium citrate is a natural form of potassium.

Pyridoxine hydrochloride is a synthetic source of vitamin B6.

Riboflavin is a synthetic source of vitamin B2.

Selenium is an essential mineral.

Sodium chloride is a synthetic form of salt—table salt.

Sodium selenite is a synthetic form of the essential mineral selenium.

Taurine is an amino acid.

Thiamine hydrochloride is a synthetic source of vitamin B1, thiamine.

Thiamine mononitrate is a synthetic source of vitamin B1.

Zinc carbonate is a source of the mineral zinc.

Zinc oxide is a natural form of the mineral zinc.

Zinc sulfate is a synthetic form of the mineral zinc.

CHART 9
SAMPLE DETAILED GUARANTEED ANALYSIS

This chart contains a sample bird food label, listing ingredients and a guaranteed analysis. This analysis includes not only protein, fat, fiber and moisture, but also minerals, vitamins and amino acids—all very necessary for your bird's continued good health. When at all possible, buy foods with a very complete label, such as this one, so that you can better compare foods and select the best food for your bird.

Sample Selected Parrot Food

Ingredients: safflower seed, sunflower seed, whole corn, pelleted parrot food, wheat, oat groats, whole peanuts, rosehips, chili peppers, soybean oil, preservatives, orange flavoring, added vitamins and minerals.

Guaranteed analysis:

Protein	16%
Fat	15%
Fiber	16%
Moisture	10%

Minerals:

calcium: minimum	.20%
maximum	.70%
phosphorus	.55%
potassium	.50%
salt: minimum	.07%
maximum	.57%
magnesium	.29%
manganese	.002%
iron	.002%
zinc	.002%
copper	.0005%
iodine	.00002%
selenium	.00001%

Vitamins (per lb.):

vitamin A	2000 IU
vitamin D3	200 IU
vitamin E	5 IU
menadione	.2 mg
thiamine	1.5 mg
riboflavin	1.2 mg
vitamin B6	3 mg
niacin	30 mg
d-pantothenic acid	9 mg
vitamin B12	.6 mcg
biotin	.01 mg
folic acid	.05 mg
choline	650 mg

Amino acids:

alanine	1%
arginine	1.45%
aspartic acid	1.3%
cystine	.6%
glutamic acid	.91%
glycine	1.05%
histidine	.4%
isoleucine	.7%
leucine	1.28%
lysine	.7%
methionine	.38%
phenylalanine	.82%
proline	.75%
serine	.58%
tryptophan	.23%
tyrosine	.50%
valine	.93%

ARTIFICIAL COLORING

Many of the artificial colorings used in pet foods have been associated with potential problems. FD & C Red No. 40 is a possible carcinogen but is widely used to keep meat looking fresh. Blue No. 2 is thought to increase some animals' sensitivity to viruses. Another color that is commonly used but has not been fully tested is Yellow No. 5. Red No. 2 and Violet No. 1 were banned by the FDA in the mid-1970s as possible carcinogens, but prior to that were widely used in pet foods.

THERE'S MORE!

Sugar is not an ingredient most people would expect to find in bird food (except in nectar formulas), but some bird foods do contain sugar. The sugar adds palatability and moistness and aids in preventing bacterial contamination. But the amount of sugar used in commercial foods is definitely not needed by most birds and can stress the pancreas and adrenal glands, causing diabetes or other problems. Completely devoid of protein, vitamins and minerals, for many birds sugar is, literally, empty calories.

Salt is added to many foods as a meat preservative. Too much salt can irritate the digestive system and can cause a mineral imbalance because the salt itself can upset the calcium-potassium balance.

REMEMBER QUALITY

The presence of some or all of the ingredients listed in this chapter, which are the most commonly used bird food ingredients, does not necessarily mean your bird is going to be well nourished. The ingredients must be in the right combinations and be of good quality, both before and after processing.

BIOLOGICAL VALUE. The biological values of the ingredients are a key to good nutrition. The biological value of a food is a measure of how complete the amino acids are in the proteins contained in the food. For example, eggs are considered a wonderful source of protein because they contain all of the essential amino acids. Therefore, eggs have a biological value of 100 percent. Fish meal has a biological value of 92 percent; beef is 78 percent, as is milk; wheat is 60 percent, wheat gluten is 40 percent; corn is 54 percent. Neither wheat nor corn would be an adequate diet alone, but fed together with one or two meat- or seed-based proteins (depending upon the species) capable of supplying the missing amino acids, they could supply an adequate diet.

DIGESTIBILITY OF FOOD. Digestibility refers to how much of the food is actually absorbed by the bird's system. The more food that is actually metabolized, the higher the digestibility. During feeding trials, the birds' feces are collected and analyzed to determine the undigested residues of the food eaten. Dr. Steve Hannah, a nutrition scientist with Purina, explains, "Digestibility is determined by the amount of food consumed by the animal, minus the amount of undigested or unabsorbed food in the stool."

High digestibility indicates that the nutrients within a given food are readily available to be used by the animal. Consideration is given, too, to the type of bird and the normal digestive processes for that bird.

QUALITY BEFORE PROCESSING. Understanding the definition of an ingredient is not enough. A short description doesn't tell us exactly how good that ingredient is. Many grains grown in poor soil will lack needed vitamins and minerals, and unfortunately, this happens quite often in the United States. Grains and vegetables can also be polluted with pesticides of various kinds and fertilizer residues, herbicides and anti-fungal sprays. Seeds and nuts can "die," losing their freshness and, in the process, much of their nutritional value.

Vegetables, fruits, seeds and nuts are often treated with substances after harvesting. For example, many grocery stores display vegetables coated with a wax. This supposedly preserves freshness and again, is supposedly harmless. But when I questioned the produce manager at a local grocery store he could tell me nothing about this wax, what it was, what it contained or any studies regarding its safety. All kinds of ingredients can also be soiled with molds, mildews and fungus.

Richard H. Pitcairn, DVM, PhD, and Susan Hubble Pitcairn, authors of *Natural Health for Dogs and Cats,* remind us of another group of additives that has been left off the pet food packages: hormones, insecticides and other chemicals. The majority of livestock used for food production is loaded with growth hormones, pesticides, antibiotics and other chemicals. Meat from the fetal tissues of pregnant cows is naturally high in hormones, and high cooking temperatures do not inactivate these hormones. There are more meat sources in bird foods than you would think. Animal fats are very prevalent, even in many seed foods.

The U.S. Department of Agriculture (USDA) does not mandate federal inspection of ingredients used in pet food manufacturing. However, some states do inspect manufacturing plants.

QUALITY AFTER PROCESSING. Many nutrients—especially enzymes and some vitamins and minerals—can be damaged by the high temperatures used in processing pet foods. If the nutrients are in the raw foods but are damaged during processing, they are obviously not going to help your pet.

CONSULT THE SOURCE

The name, address and phone number of the manufacturer should be on the label of every bird food you buy, so you can contact the manufacturer if you have any questions about the product. Make sure you have the bag of food, the can or box in front of you when you call, because the representative will ask for the product code.

IN CLOSING

Bird food labels do provide quite a bit of information, and learning how to decipher it can take some time. However, the time to do that is not when you're in a hurry, standing in the store aisle looking at all the foods available. Instead, study the labels at your leisure. You might even buy a variety of foods (or ask if samples are available) so that you can compare the labels at home and, more important, so that you can see if your bird is even attracted to the food.

As you study, keep in mind that much information is left off the label, such as the quality of the ingredients used. As we know, that information can be very difficult to come by. But feel free to call the manufacturer and ask to speak with someone who can answer your questions. In the end, make your decision based upon your understanding of the label, the recommendations of experts, including your veterinarian, the philosophy and reputation of the company, and the price of the food itself.

CHART 10
COMMERCIAL BIRD SEED COMPARISONS

This chart does not include all the bird seed foods available; in fact, it touches on only a few of the foods available through pet supply stores and other suppliers. However, this chart does show you comparisons between various foods, so you can see how to make similar comparisons that enable you to choose the right food for your bird.

FINCHES

Product	Ingredients
Hartz Total Diet for Finches Protein 11.5% Fat 2.5% Fiber 8% Moisture 12%	First five ingredients (in order): white millet, canary grass seed, red millet, vitamin and mineral concentrate, added vitamins and minerals
Hartz Vitamin and Mineral Enriched Finch Seed Protein 10.5% Fat 2% Fiber 8% Moisture 10.5%	First five ingredients (in order): millet seed, red millet seed, canary grass seed, mineral oil, manganese gluconate Other ingredients of note: added vitamins and minerals
Kaytee Perfect Choice Fortified Premium Finch Food Protein 14% Fat 9% Fiber 10% Moisture 12%	Seed mixture: red millet, yellow millet, oat groats, niger seed, flax seed, canary grass seed, rape seed, sesame seed, lettuce seed Other ingredients of note: dehydrated carrots, oyster shell, coconut, dehydrated spinach, dehydrated alfalfa, added vitamins and minerals

CHART 10, CONTINUED, FINCHES

Product	Ingredients
Nutriphase Finch Formula Protein 14% Fat 5% Fiber 8% Moisture 12%	Seed mixture: white millet, small yellow millet, red millet, canary grass seed, oat groats, niger seed, rape seed, flax seed Other ingredients of note: pelleted foods made from corn gluten meal, dehulled soybean meal, wheat middlings, dried whey and more; added vitamins and minerals
United Pacific Supreme Finch Mix Protein 12% Fat 5% Fiber 9% Ash 6% Moisture 12%	Seed mixture: small yellow millet, white millet, red millet, canary grass seed, oats, flax seed, rape seed, niger seed

CANARIES

Product	Ingredients
Hartz Total Diet for Canaries Protein 14.4% Fat 9% Fiber 8% Moisture 12%	First five ingredients (in order): canary grass seed, white millet, rape seed, vitamin and mineral concentrate, added vitamins and minerals Other ingredients of note: flax seed, cut oats, red millet, soy flour
Hartz Vitamin and Mineral Enriched Master Canary Food Protein 14% Fat 9% Fiber 8% Moisture 10%	First five ingredients (in order): millet seed, canary grass seed, rape seed, flax seed, soy flour Other ingredients of note: added vitamins and minerals

Product	Ingredients
Nutriphase Canary Formula Protein 17% Fat 11% Fiber 8% Moisture 12%	First five ingredients (in order): canary grass seed, rape seed, niger seed, oat groats, small yellow millet Other ingredients of note: white and red millet, flax seed, corn, soybean meal, dried whey, brewer's dried yeast, added vitamins and minerals

BUDGERIGARS (PARAKEETS)

Product	Ingredients
AlphaPet Parakeet Seed Protein 10% Fat 3% Fiber 8% Moisture 12%	First five ingredients (in order): white millet, sunflower seed, oat groats, canary grass seed, hulled oat groats Other ingredients of note: added vitamins and minerals
Amazon Smythe Fortified Parakeet Food Protein 14% Fat 4% Fiber 8% Moisture 12%	First five ingredients (in order): canary grass seed, white millet, oat groats, red millet, flax seed Other ingredients of note: corn, rice, dried whey, added vitamins and minerals
Hartz Vitamin and Mineral Enriched Parakeet Seed Protein 10% Fat 2% Fiber 9% Moisture 12%	First five ingredients (in order): millet seed, oat groats, canary grass seed, iodized salt, mineral oil Other ingredients of note: added vitamins and minerals

CHART 10, CONTINUED, BUDGERIGARS

Product	Ingredients
Kaytee Perchmate Vitamin and Mineral Enriched Food for Parakeets Protein 14% Fat 4% Fiber 8% Moisture 12%	Seed mixture: white millet, canary grass seed, red millet, oat groats, rape seed, buckwheat Other ingredients of note: dehulled soybean meal, corn gluten meal, wheat middlings, dried whey, added vitamins and minerals
Nutriphase Parakeet Formula Protein 14% Fat 4% Fiber 8% Moisture 12%	First five ingredients (in order): white millet, canary grass seed, oat groats, red millet, flax seed Other ingredients of note: ground corn, oyster shell, ground rice, dried whey, dehydrated alfalfa meal, brewer's yeast, added vitamins and minerals
United Pacific Supreme Parakeet Mix Protein 12% Fat 3.5% Fiber 9% Ash 3.5% Moisture 13%	Seed mixture: millet, canary grass seed, oat groats

COCKATIELS

Product	Ingredients
Amazon Smythe Fortified Cockatiel Food Protein 15% Fat 8% Fiber 14% Moisture 12%	First five ingredients (in order): white millet, canary grass seed, striped sunflower seed, safflower, oat groats Other ingredients of note: red millet, toasted corn flakes, flax

Amazon Smythe, Continued

seed, wheat, cantaloupe seed, and more; added vitamins and minerals; some dehydrated fruits and vegetables, including alfalfa meal and papaya

Hagen Cockatiel Vitamin and Mineral Enriched Formula

Protein	13%
Fat	10%
Fiber	13%
Moisture	12%

First five ingredients (in order): sunflower seed, white millet, oat groats, oats, canary grass seed
Other ingredients of note: red millet, added vitamins and minerals

Hagen Gourmet Seed-Fruit-Vegetable Mix for Cockatiels

Protein	12%
Fat	10%
Fiber	9%
Moisture	9%

First five ingredients (in order): red millet, oat groats, white millet, flax seed, sunflower seed
Other ingredients of note: flaked corn, canary grass seed, whole wheat, green split peas, Tropican extruded granules, pumpkin seed, raisins, dehydrated pineapple, dehydrated carrot, green bell peppers, peanuts, added vitamins and minerals

Hartz Total Diet for Cockatiels

Protein	13%
Fat	8%
Pelleted fiber	7%
Moisture	12%

Seed mixture: oat groats, dehulled cracked sunflower seed, white millet, red millet
Other ingredients of note: food containing hulled millet, added vitamins and minerals

CHART 10, CONTINUED
PARROTS, MACAWS, COCKATOOS AND OTHER LARGE HOOKBILLS

Product	Ingredients
8 in 1 Parrot Ultra-Blend Advanced Nutrition Diet Protein 16% Fat 15% Fiber 16% Moisture 10% Vitamin A 2000 IU/lb.	First five ingredients (in order): safflower seed, sunflower seed, whole corn, pelleted parrot food, wheat Other ingredients of note: oat groats, peanuts, rosehips, chili peppers, added vitamins and minerals
Lafeber's Nutri-Berries Macaw-Cockatoo Food Protein 11% Fat 6% Fiber 4% Moisture 14%	First five ingredients (in order): cracked corn, hulled white millet, peanuts, oat groats, malto-dextrin Other ingredients of note: canary grass seed, safflower, corn oil, whole egg, added vitamins and minerals
Nutriphase Parrot Formula Protein 16% Fat 14% Fiber 20% Moisture 12% Vitamin A (minimum) 2500 IU/lb.	First five ingredients (in order): striped sunflower seed, safflower, oat groats, corn, wheat Other ingredients of note: peanuts, red peppers, dried bananas, oyster shell, rice, pumpkin seed, added vitamins and minerals
United Pacific Supreme Parrot Mix Protein 17.5% Fat 23.5% Fiber 28% Moisture 9%	First five ingredients (in order): sunflower seed, peanuts, whole yellow corn, hard red wheat, popcorn Other ingredients of note: pumpkin seed, chili peppers

DOVES

Product	Ingredients

Kaytee Dove Food
Universal Supreme
    Protein   10%
    Fat   2%
    Fiber   3%
    Moisture   12%
	First three ingredients (in order): milo, kaffir, wheat

CHART 11
COMMERCIAL PELLETED BIRD
FOOD COMPARISONS

This chart does not list all the bird foods available—not by any means. Instead, this list shows you some of the available foods, how they compare to each other and how you can compare other foods. These comparisons can help you decide what food may be best for your bird.

MYNAHS

Product	First Five Ingredients

8 in 1 Pet Products
Tasty Dinner with Fruit
for Mynahs
    Protein   25%
    Fat   7%
    Fiber   4%
    Moisture   10%
	Apple, peach, orange, yellow corn, soybean meal
	Other ingredients of note: meat meal, dried cheese meal, brewer's yeast, added vitamins, minerals and trace minerals

CHART 11, CONTINUED
COCKATIELS

Product	First Five Ingredients
Kaytee Exact Rainbow Complete Daily Diet for Cockatiels	Ground corn, ground wheat, ground oat groats, wheat middlings, corn gluten meal
Protein 14% Fat 5% Fiber 5% Moisture 12%	Other ingredients of note: dried whole egg, dried beet pulp, soybean meal, corn oil, wheat germ meal, added vitamins and minerals
Lafeber's Premium Daily Diet for Cockatiels	Ground corn, wheat, steamed rolled oats, soybean meal, molasses
Protein 14% Fat 4% Fiber 2% Moisture 10.5%	Other ingredients of note: dried whole egg, added vitamins and minerals

PARROTS, COCKATOOS, MACAWS AND OTHER HOOKBILLS

Product	First Five Ingredients
Kaytee Exact Original Complete Daily Diet for Parrots and Conures	Ground corn, ground wheat, ground oat groats, wheat middlings, corn gluten meal
Protein 15% Fat 6% Fiber 5% Moisture 12%	Other ingredients of note: dried whole egg, dried beet pulp, added vitamins and minerals
Lafeber's Premium Daily Diet for Parrots	Ground corn, wheat, steamed rolled oats, soybean meal, molasses
Protein 14% Fat 4% Fiber 2% Moisture 10.5%	Other ingredients of note: dried whole egg, added vitamins and minerals

HAND FEEDING FOODS

Product	First Five Ingredients
Kaytee Exact Original Hand Feeding Formula Protein 22% Fat 8% Fiber 5% Moisture 10%	Ground corn, corn gluten meal, ground oat groats, ground wheat, wheat middlings Other ingredients of note: dried whole egg, brewer's yeast, dried bacillus species, added vitamins and minerals
Kellogg Peep Nestling Food with Egg Protein 15% Fat 45% Fiber 5% Moisture 11%	Bread crumbs, ground yellow corn, oat groats, soybean meal, feeding oatmeal Other ingredients of note: hemp seed, niger seed, dried whole egg, dehydrated alfalfa meal, brewer's yeast, soybean oil, added vitamins and minerals

SEVEN

CHOOSING THE RIGHT
COMMERCIAL FOOD

There are quite a few different bird foods available to pet owners, with more appearing each year. There are seed mixtures, suet blocks, seed and dehydrated vegetable mixtures, pelleted foods and hard stick treats. Some foods are incredibly expensive and others are very cheap. There are very nutritious, complete foods made with ingredients approved for human use and other foods of dubious nutritional value with very questionable ingredients. Some foods are nationally advertised, while others are known in small geographical areas and promoted by word of mouth.

How can you sift through this cornucopia of foods and narrow the field down to one? Again, knowledge is the key: knowledge of the foods, what they are and what the terms mean.

FORMS OF FOODS AND THEIR PROS AND CONS

Most bird foods come in one of eight different forms:

- seed mixes
- seed mixes with other ingredients
- pelleted foods
- hard sticks or bars
- natural foods
- suet
- live insects
- nectar

SEED MIXES. Seed mixes are the oldest form of bird food, the most traditional, and still the most popular. Seed mixes can be found in grocery stores, pet supply stores, even hardware and discount stores.

Pros: Seed mixes are convenient.

Cons: Seeds alone rarely satisfy all of the nutritional needs of even seed-eating birds. Seeds alone lack several key nutrients, including vitamin A, D, B12, calcium, trace minerals and some amino acids.

Also, seeds can spoil, "die" or become infested with weevils. In researching this book, I bought boxed seeds from several types of stores, including discount stores, and most of the boxed (rather than bagged) seeds were infested with weevils, some terribly so.

SEED MIXES WITH OTHER INGREDIENTS. Seed mixes can now be found with a variety of other ingredients included. Pelleted foods, food flakes, dehydrated vegetables or fruits, chopped or diced nuts, gravel or grit, as well as added vitamins and minerals might be included.

Pros: These foods are more likely to satisfy a bird's nutritional needs than seed mixtures alone. The variety of ingredients can also make eating more stimulating for the bird, hopefully reducing cage boredom.

Cons: These foods can spoil and should be stored in a closed, airtight container. Some of these foods are preserved with questionable preservatives; make sure you read the labels.

PELLETED FOODS. Several different manufacturers make pelleted foods using several different processes. When choosing a pelleted food, make sure you read the labels carefully. What are the ingredients? What is the nutritional value of the food? If you have any questions, call the manufacturer.

Pros: Good-quality manufactured, pelleted foods can be very good nutrition for your bird, easily digested and palatable.

Cons: It can sometimes be difficult to change an adult bird over to a pelleted food. Many breeders start feeding baby birds pelleted foods right after weaning. These birds will then accept pelleted foods all their lives. Adult birds, however, can resist this change and sometimes never recognize the pelleted food as food.

Pelleted foods may contain preservatives, artificial colorings and/or flavorings. Make sure you read the label and are comfortable with the ingredients of the food.

HARD STICKS OR BARS. Hard sticks or bars are usually sold as treats and can easily become part of a bird's diet. They are usually made of seeds or seeds and nuts, glued together with gelatin, gelatin and honey, or another ingredient that will help bind the ingredients together.

Pros: These sticks and bars provide good beak and chewing exercise for the bird, as well as additional nutrition.

Cons: They are not nutritionally complete foods and should not be fed as such. In no case should these treats make up more than 10 percent of the bird's diet.

CHART 12
NUTRITIONAL COMPARISONS OF BIRD TREATS

This chart does not list all the bird treats available—not by any means. Instead, this list shows you some of the available foods, how they compare with each other and how you can compare other foods. These comparisons can help you decide what food may be best for your bird.

BUDGERIGARS (PARAKEETS)

Product	First Five Ingredients (in order)
Hartz Parakeet Fortified Oats 'N Groats Protein 14% Fat 5% Fiber 3.5% Moisture 10%	Oat groats, natural anise flavor, dl-alpha tocopherol acetate (source of vitamin E), corn oil, vitamin A palmitate
Hartz Condition Treat for Parakeets, Cockatiels, Canaries and Finches Protein 10% Fat 2% Fiber 5% Moisture 10%	Millet seed, red millet seed, oat groats, corn grits, dried carrots Other ingredients of note: dehydrated apples, tomatoes, celery, apricots, oranges, lemons, prunes, other fruits and vegetables, added vitamins and minerals, artificial colors and flavorings
Hartz Fruit 'N Nut Snack for Parakeets Protein 14.5% Fat 12% Fiber 6% Moisture 10%	Millet seed, red millet seed, oat groats, rape seed, canary grass seed Other ingredients of note: sunflower seed, soya nuts, flax seed, hazelnuts, walnuts, pecans,

Product	First Five Ingredients (in order)
Hartz Fruit 'N Nut Snack, Continued	dehydrated apples, oranges, prunes, apricots, lemons, added vitamins and minerals, artificial colorings
Hartz Parakeet High Energy Blend Protein 13.5% Fat 8% Fiber 5.5% Moisture 10%	Millet seed, oat groats, flax seed, canary grass seed, red millet Other ingredients of note: natural and artificial flavorings and colors, added vitamins and minerals
Kaytee Gourmet Fruit & Vegetable Treat for Parakeets Protein 15% Fat 12% Fiber 10% Moisture 12%	Dehydrated carrots, canary grass seed, niger seed, oat groats, small yellow millet Other ingredients of note: dehydrated apples, prunes, parsley, spinach, orange peel, alfalfa meal, added vitamins and minerals, red millet, flax seed, rice, hemp seed, pearled barley and more
LM Animal Farms Fruit Cocktail for Parakeets Protein 13% Fat 8% Fiber 6.8% Moisture 10.3%	White millet, red millet, canary grass seed, oat groats, flax seed Other ingredients of note: rape seed, sesame seed, niger seed, anise seed, dehydrated oranges, apples, carrots, parsley, alfalfa meal, meat and bone meal, fish meal, and more; added vitamins and minerals
Vitakraft Kiwi Fruit Sticks Protein 9% Fat 2.6% Fiber 8.7% Moisture 9.6%	Yellow millet, panicum millet, spray millet, toasted wheat, flour Other ingredients of note: kiwi, honey, added vitamins and minerals
Vitakraft Banana Sticks Protein 10.4% Fat 3.3% Fiber 5.9% Moisture not listed	Yellow millet, panicum millet, spray millet, toasted wheat flour, banana Other ingredients of note: red millet, honey, added vitamins and minerals

CHART 12, CONTINUED
BUDGERIGARS

Product	First Five Ingredients (in order)
Vitakraft Sticks with Egg	Golden millet, panicum millet, spray millet, eggs, toasted wheat flour
Protein 10%	
Fat 2.8%	
Fiber 5.7%	Other ingredients of note: honey, niger seed, yeast, added vitamins and minerals
Moisture not listed	
Vitakraft Sticks with Honey	Golden millet, panicum millet, spray millet, toasted wheat flour, calcium phosphate
Protein 9.4%	
Fat 2.9%	
Fiber 9.1%	Other ingredients of note: honey, added vitamins and minerals
Moisture 8.7%	

CANARIES

Product	First Five Ingredients (in order)
Kaytee Molting, Conditioning and Color Food Complement for Canaries and Finches	Dehulled soybean meal, oat groats, corn grits, niger seed, canary grass seed, corn gluten meal
	Other ingredients of note:
Protein 21%	rape seed, red millet, yellow millet,
Fat 8%	white millet, flax seed, poppy seed,
Fiber 8%	added vitamins and minerals, dehy-
Moisture 12%	drated alfalfa, parsley and carrots

COCKATIELS

Product	First Five Ingredients
8 in 1 Ultra-Blend Honey Bars for Cockatiels	Safflower seeds, white millet, sunflower seeds, red millet, oat groats
Protein 17.5%	Other ingredients of note:
Fat 9.5%	granulated cockatiel food,
Fiber 15%	added vitamins and minerals, dried
Moisture 13%	whole eggs, artificial colors

Product	First Five Ingredients
Kaytee Fruit & Vegetable Treat Stick	Canary grass seed, safflower, sunflower, white millet, oat groats
Protein 13% Fat 10% Fiber 15% Moisture 12%	Other ingredients of note: dehydrated apples, carrots, raisins, cherries, sweet potatoes, raspberries, alfalfa meal, added vitamins and minerals, dried whey, brewer's yeast, hemp seed, niger seed and more
LM Animal Farms Grains & Honey for Cockatiels	Pumpkin seed, safflower seed, raisins, juniper berries, mountain ash berries
Protein 15.8% Fat 10.5% Fiber 8.5% Moisture 9.5%	Other ingredients of note: honey, cracked corn, corn puffs, corn nuts, sunflower, peanuts, hemp seed, flax seed and more; dehydrated bananas, oranges, papaya, apple and more
Orange Blossom Honey Treat for Cockatiels	Canary grass seed, white millet, safflower, sunflower seed, flax seed
Protein 14% Fat 10% Fiber 12% Moisture 12%	Other ingredients of note: canary grass seed, white millet, safflower seed, sunflower seed, flax seed, rape seed, wheat, oat groats, millet, amaranth, hemp, rice and more; added vitamins and minerals

FINCHES

Product	First Five Ingredients
LM Animal Farms Fruit Cocktail for Finches	German millet, red millet, white millet, canary grass seed, flax seed
Protein 13% Fat 10.5% Fiber 7.7% Moisture 7.5%	Other ingredients of note: rape seed niger seed, sesame seed, poppy seed, anise seed, dehydrated oranges, apples, carrots, parsley, alfalfa and more; added vitamins and minerals

CHART 12, CONTINUED
PARROTS

Product	First Five Ingredients (in order)
Gourmet Fruit & Vegetable Treat for Parrots	Safflower, raisins, sunflower, dried bananas, dehydrated carrots
Protein 14%	Other ingredients of note:
Fat 8%	dehydrated alfalfa meal, papaya,
Fiber 14%	peas, sweet potatoes, peppers,
Moisture 12%	parsley, apples, dates, prunes, peaches, pumpkin seed, hemp seed and more; added vitamins and minerals
Kaytee Nutra-Puffs Tropical Fruit Flavored Treat	Corn flour, salt, calcium carbonate, vitamin A supplement, choline
Protein 7.5%	chloride
Fat .5%	Other ingredients of note: added
Fiber 2%	itamins and minerals, artificial
Moisture 12%	colors, natural flavorings
Kaytee Fruit & Vegetable Treat Stick	Sunflower, safflower, canary grass seed, white millet, wheat
Protein 13%	Other ingredients of note:
Fat 12%	dehydrated apples, dehydrated
Fiber 18%	carrots, raisins, dried bananas,
Moisture 12%	oat groats, popcorn, pearled barley, buckwheat, red millet, hemp seed, dehydrated cherries, dehydrated sweet potatoes, added vitamins and minerals, and more
Kaytee Tropical Fruit Treat for Parrots	Safflower, sunflower, white millet, oat groats, canary grass seed
Protein 14%	Other ingredients of note:
Fat 12%	dehydrated or dried banana, papaya,
Fiber 14%	mango, raisins, dates, figs,
Moisture 12%	pineapple and more; whole egg, beet pulp, fish meal and more; added vitamins and minerals

NATURAL FOODS. Some commercial bird foods come in a natural form. Spray millet, for example, is dried millet still on the stem. Cuttlefish bone is dried and processed but arrives on the store shelf in a natural form.

Other natural foods are foods you eat that you can also feed your bird, such as vegetables, fruits, nuts, grain products and so on.

Pros: Natural foods are often more recognizable as foods to many birds. Natural, unprocessed foods are often more easily digested, too.

Cons: When feeding a diet comprised of natural foods, you need to do more work to ensure that the diet is complete and balanced. You should feed a vitamin and mineral supplement to make sure all the bird's needs are met.

SUET. Suet foods are made from rendered beef fat and mixed with other ingredients, usually nuts and/or berries or fruit. Suet is a very nutritious, high-fat, high-calorie food that can be very beneficial to wild birds. You can also feed suet (sparingly!) to pet birds during times of stress, recuperation or illness.

Pros: Suet can be very nutritious in certain situations.

Cons: Suet can be purchased pre-made, but even then it can be very messy to handle and feed. It is very high in calories and can cause obesity in pet birds if fed too much or too often.

LIVE FOODS. Birds that require insects as part (or almost all) of their diet will need to eat live insects.

Pros: Insects can be purchased at most pet supply stores or from mail order companies (see Chart 6).

Cons: Insects themselves must first be fed before you give them to your bird, to ensure that the insects offer good nutrition. Insects can escape into your house, so you must be able to give the insects to your bird in such a way that as few as possible escape.

NECTAR. Orioles, hummingbirds and lories all require nectar or sugar water. Although these first two birds are rarely kept as pets, lories are and can do quite well in captivity.

Pros: A proper nectar solution can provide good nutrition to lories, although many experts do recommend additional foods to supplement the nectar to ensure good nutrition.

Cons: A liquid nectar diet requires work from the bird's owner; mixing the solution, cleaning the supplies and feeders regularly and cleaning the bird's cage. A liquid diet results in very liquid droppings, often released in a projectile manner—a mess!

MIXING FOODS

Many bird owners regularly mix foods to provide a varied diet. For example, you might try mixing chopped vegetables, a few fruits and some soaked dry pelleted food.

Many experts believe a mixture may be the best choice for many birds because the variety can better ensure a higher biological value of the total food consumed. However, when putting together a diet of various foods, you must take care to ensure that all of the foods are high quality and are appropriate to the specific bird or species.

CHART 13
BIRD FOOD TASTE TESTS

To compare the palatability and acceptance of some commonly available bird foods, I used my birds and my friends' birds. The birds were used to trying a variety of foods and were not finicky eaters.

To conduct the cockatiel and parrot taste tests, I first got each bird acquainted with being on the kitchen counter. Then I spread the foods out on the counter in front of the bird, at equal distances. I noted each bird's reactions to the various foods.

For the finch and budgerigar tests I placed five different food dishes in the birds' cages. I measured the amount of food I put in and measured what was left 24 hours later.

Clearly, these tests are not scientific; however, it is interesting to note the birds' reactions to the foods.

Cockatiel Foods and Treats
Foods offered:
    Hagen Gourmet Seed-Fruit-Vegetable Mix
    Hagen Staple VME Seeds for Cockatiels
    Hartz Total Diet for Cockatiels
    Kaytee Orange Blossom Honey Treat for Cockatiels
    LM Animal Farms Grains and Honey for Cockatiels

Results: Pretty Bird, a lovely young cockatiel, was thrilled with the selection of foods and went back and forth, chittering with happiness, testing several different foods before settling herself in front of the LM Animal Farms Grains and Honey.

Parrot Foods and Treats

Foods offered:
  Kaytee Fruit & Vegetable Treat Stick
  United Pacific Supreme Parrot Mix
  Nutriphase Parrot Formula
  Kaytee Exact Original Complete Daily Diet (softened)
  8 in 1 Pet Products Parrot Ultra-Blend

Results: Bingo, an African Grey, nibbled some sunflower seeds from the Ultra-Blend, then from the Supreme food. She then munched some peanuts before finally grabbing the treat stick and starting to vigorously eat it.

Finch Foods and Treats

Foods offered:
  Kaytee Perfect Choice Finch Food
  United Pacific Supreme Finch Mix
  Nutriphase Finch Formula
  Hartz Finch Seed
  LM Animal Farms Fruit Cocktail for Finches

Results: The pair of Zebra finches was very enthusiastic about the LM Animal Farms mixture, eating over two-thirds of the dish of food, compared to less than one-half of each of the other foods.

Budgerigar (Parakeet) Foods

Foods offered:
  Hartz High Energy Blend
  Hartz Parakeet Seed
  Kaytee Perchmate Seed for Parakeets
  United Pacific Supreme Parakeet Mix
  Nutriphase Parakeet Formula

Results: The pair of budgies was enthusiastic about the Nutriphase food, eating two-thirds of the food. Next most popular was the Hartz High Energy Blend.

EIGHT

SUPPLEMENTS: SHOULD YOU OR SHOULDN'T YOU?

Most nutritionists and veterinarians consider a supplement to be anything that is regularly added to the bird's diet. Should you use supplements? As with so many aspects of bird nutrition, the experts' opinions vary. Some say a good quality food (or diet) is all a bird needs. Many of the commercial bird food manufacturers state that their food is "complete and balanced" and needs no supplementation. However, many other experts say that even a "complete and balanced" bird food is not always enough, that it doesn't take into consideration each species' needs, each individual bird's needs or the actual quality and digestibility of the diet.

Dr. Clarence Hardin, the director of the California Mobile Veterinary Service and a respected preventive medicine vet, is in favor of dietary supplements. He says, "Today's pets face a number of critical health dangers, including air and water pollution and sub-standard, chemically laden foods. Often traditional nutrition and medicine is not enough."

DECIDING TO SUPPLEMENT

Deciding what supplements to add to your bird's diet can be difficult. Some bird owners might see an advertisement for a new product that is supposed to be on the "cutting edge" of nutrition and decide to try it, while other bird owners might hear or read about a supplement that is supposed to accomplish something specific, such as produce healthy bones, and they decide to try it. Other bird owners do a lot of research, searching out exactly the right nutrients for their bird.

As long as the supplement itself is appropriate to the bird species, is not harmful to the bird and is given in an amount appropriate to the bird's size, condition and general health, a supplement poses no real danger except that it may unbalance a previously balanced, complete food or diet. On the other hand, not giving a supplement could seriously endanger your bird's health. If you have any questions or doubts, call the manufacturer of the food your bird is eating, the manufacturer of the supplement you are thinking of using, and your bird's veterinarian. Then, with all the various opinions, it will still be up to you: Should you or shouldn't you?

THE DANGERS OF SUPPLEMENTS

When giving supplements, it is important to closely watch your bird's overall condition and health. If there appears to be any kind of allergic reaction, stop the supplement and call your veterinarian. If there is any detrimental change in your bird's condition or health, again, stop the supplement and talk to your veterinarian.

Keep in mind that in the wild, the fittest survive. Those that are sick or weak do not survive, or do not survive as long. Therefore, our birds are genetically programmed to hide weaknesses for as long as possible. However, if you know your bird and watch it closely, you will be able to see problems and step in before they get too serious.

COMMERCIALLY AVAILABLE SUPPLEMENTS

VITAMIN AND MINERAL SUPPLEMENTS. There are probably as many vitamin and mineral supplements available for birds as there are for people. There are complete vitamin and mineral preparations, vitamin-only supplements and mineral-only supplements.

If you are feeding a seed mixture diet, or a seed mixture diet with vegetables and fruits added, it is safe to give your bird a vitamin and mineral supplement. If you are feeding a pelleted commercial diet that advertises itself as complete and balanced, you may not have to supplement the diet at all.

CHART 14
VITAMINS AND SUPPLEMENTS

This chart contains a very small sample of the bird supplements available. Use these comparisons as a guide to reading the labels on any supplements you may want to use. Ask yourself these questions: What is the supplement supposed to do? What is in it? What is the analysis? Can this supplement potentially do what I'd like it to do?

8 in 1 Pet Products Iron and Blood Supplement

Ingredients: water, ferrous gluconate, dextrose, potassium sorbate

Analysis: 0.186% iron, from ferrous gluconate

8 in 1 Pet Products Skin and Plumage Food Supplement

Ingredients: soybean oil, cod liver oil, lecithin, wheat germ oil, mono- and diglycerides of fatty acids, propyl paraben (a preservative), vitamin A palmitate, cholecalciferol, dl-alpha tocopherol acetate, BHT and propyl gallate (as preservatives)

Analysis (per fluid ounce):

Vitamin A	7,800 IU
Vitamin D3	1,550 IU
Vitamin E	2.5 IU
Linoleic acid	13,500 mg
Linolenic acid	1,200 mg
Oleic acid	6,500 mg
Choline	18 mg
Inositol	10 mg

Lambert Kay Avimin

Ingredients: water, calcium borogluconate, sodium gluconate, calcium oxide, manganese gluconate, zinc gluconate, copper gluconate, potassium iodide, artificial coloring, preservatives (potassium sorbate, methylparaben, polyparaben)

Analysis (per ml):

Calcium	13 mg
Sodium	6 mg

Zinc	250 mcg
Manganese	150 mcg
Copper	65 mcg
Iodine	1.5 mcg

Mardel Laboratories VitaFlight

Ingredients: dextrose, niacinamide, vitamin A supplement, menadione sodium bisulfate complex (source of vitamin K activity), calcium pantothenate, dl-alpha tocopherol acetate (source of vitamin E), d-activated animal sterol (source of vitamin D3), riboflavin, thiamine mononitrate, vitamin B12 supplement, pyridoxine hydrochloride, folic acid, biotin, BHT and ethoxyquin (as preservatives)

Analysis (per kg):

Vitamin A	3,960,000 IU
Vitamin D3	1,975,000 IU
Vitamin E	2,000 IU
Riboflavin	1,500 mg
Pantothenic acid	5,000 mg
Niacin	13,200 mg
Choline bitartrate	6,600 mg
Vitamin B6	660 mg
Menadione	5,250 mg
Thiamine	660 mg

Oasis Vita-Drops

Ingredients: vitamin A, vitamin D, vitamin E, cyanocobalamin, riboflavin 5-phosphate, niacin, menadione SMC, folic acid, choline chloride, sodium benzoate, water

Analysis:

Vitamin A	3,027 IU
Vitamin D	180 IU
Vitamin E	1 IU
Vitamin B12	10 mcg
Riboflavin	3 mcg
Niacin	3 mg
Pantothenic acid	1 mg

CHART 14, Continued
VITAMINS AND SUPPLEMENTS

Analysis continued:

Menadione	1 mcg
Folic acid	14 mcg
Thiamine monotrate	60 mg
Pyridoxine hydrochloride	15 mcg
Choline chloride	26 mg
Vitamin C	18 mg
Vitamin K	7 mcg

Special Supplements. Some supplements are supposed to deal with one or more particular areas of the bird's health. Avimin by Lambert Kay is a liquid mineral supplement that advertises it supplies the essential minerals needed for growth and reproduction. Skin and Plumage Food Supplement by 8 in 1 Pet Products is made from wheat germ oil, cod liver oil and soybean oil and is supposed to supply needed fatty acids. Iron and Blood Supplement by 8 in 1 Pet Products is supposed to supply iron to correct anemia or other iron deficiencies.

Calcium and Phosphorus. Calcium-phosphorus imbalances cause problems during breeding season, when the female bird must produce enough calcium for her eggs. A cuttlefish bone in her cage is usually enough of a supplement; however, some birds need more. If you suspect your bird might have a mineral imbalance, talk to your avian veterinarian before adding more calcium-phosphorus to your bird's diet.

Enzyme Formulas. Enzyme formulas are designed to enhance or replace naturally occurring enzymes. These formulas are usually added to aid digestion. Most enzyme supplements are derived from plant sources, such as papain or bromelain. Because enzymes work in conjunction with other body processes, enzyme supplements should not be added to any bird's diet without first consulting a veterinarian experienced in avian nutrition.

If your veterinarian recommends an enzyme supplement, there are several on the market. One popular formula, Prozyme, is advertised as "Enhancing the bioavailability of all pet foods." It is supposed to work directly on the food by replacing the natural enzymes lost due to processing.

FOOD SUPPLEMENTS. A few supplements are available that are made from foods rather than simpler food forms, such as vitamins, minerals, fatty acids or enzymes. Most of these supplements are designed to provide more complete nutrition for pets, boosting what might otherwise be a less-than-complete diet.

#1 All Systems, a company known for its pet grooming products, has produced a supplement called Vital Energy. Made from flax seed, molasses, yeast, rice bran, liver, alfalfa and a number of other quality ingredients, Vital Energy contains antioxidants, phytochemicals, enzymes, amino acids, trace minerals and vitamins. Vital Energy is itself a balanced food, eliminating the concern of over-supplementation.

USING SUPPLEMENTS

Many avian vitamin formulations are designed to be mixed into the bird's water. This works well for some birds, but not so well for others. How can you tell how much your bird has actually ingested? What if your bird refuses to drink the doctored water?

A much more effective way to give supplements is to mix them with a food you know your bird likes to eat. If your bird loves bananas, mash the supplement into a piece of banana. If your bird treasures chicken or pasta, sprinkle the supplement over a tiny piece.

MAKING YOUR DECISION

Adding a supplement to your bird's food is a personal decision that should not be taken lightly. Too much supplementation can upset a previously balanced and complete diet. For example, as discussed in Chapter Four, a calcium and phosphorus imbalance can result in many potentially lethal health problems.

However, supplements added to the diet wisely can greatly benefit your bird. The key to using supplements is to do so intelligently, researching the supplement and the food your bird eats. If you have any doubts, talk to the bird food manufacturer; if the supplement you are adding is manufactured commercially, talk to that company's representative as well. If you see any detrimental changes in your bird's health, of course stop the supplement immediately and call your veterinarian.

NINE

FEEDING YOUR BIRD

This may seem like the simplest and most obvious part of providing for your bird's nutritional needs, but it, too, can be confusing. There are choices to be made about:

- how to feed your bird
- when to feed
- where to feed
- how much to feed
- how often to feed
- how to evaluate the food
- what to do when you wish to change foods

All of these things contribute to your bird's health.

HOW TO FEED?

With most birds, all you need to do is put the food in front of them. If your bird eats insects, you can offer them in a small, shallow bowl or plastic lid, such as a peanut butter jar lid. Or you can offer insects directly from your fingers.

Seeds, seed mixtures, pelleted foods and other foods can be fed in bowls or, preferably, in food holders that fasten on the side of the cage. If the bowl is too big, the bird might sit in the seed instead of on the side of the bowl or on the perch, and may defecate in the food.

Many bird keepers like to have separate food holders for each type of food. For example, a seed mixture could go in one, a treat in another and some fruit in a third. A fourth could have water.

Small birds generally will eat out of their bowl and leave it at that. However, many large birds look upon their food bowl as both a source of food and a play toy. Bowls get chewed on, thrown around, dumped and sometimes even broken. To combat this, there are food bowls on the market made specifically for large birds. Some of the bowls fasten to the cage with wing nuts or clamps. Some mount outside the cage. Look for advertisements for some of these products in bird magazines or at your local pet supply store.

WHEN TO FEED?

Some smaller birds, such as finches and canaries, must have food available to them at all times. These tiny birds have a very fast metabolism and can literally starve to death within a day. Nectar eaters are the same way, and must have food available at all times.

For safety's sake, most bird experts recommend leaving a seed mixture available to all seed-eating birds at all times. Additional foods may be given at other times during the day. For example, you may offer a bit of fruit in the morning, perhaps a piece of whole grain bread in the afternoon and a bit of chicken and pasta at night.

WHERE TO FEED?

Most birds eat where they live: in their cage, aviary or enclosure. The room where the bird is eating should be relatively quiet. If there is too much activity, the bird may pay more attention to the activity around it than to its food.

Eating is very important to birds, both physically and psychologically, so you may want to feed a certain amount of food by hand. By taking your bird out of its cage (when possible and safe) and hand feeding it, you are establishing a relationship of trust. You can teach parrots, conures, macaws, African Greys, mynahs and even budgies to rest on a chair arm or table while you hand feed some treats.

Those birds that might not be safe out of their cage can still learn to take food from your fingers. Finches, for example, will come to take a tiny mealworm.

HOW MUCH TO FEED?

This can be a difficult question to answer and is the question asked most often of experienced bird keepers and veterinarians. Obesity is a growing problem with birds and many have died of obesity-related health problems.

There is, unfortunately, no standard of how much food any one bird of any particular species should eat. Factors include the bird's species and type, activity level, environment (including temperature), the bird's age, state of health and more. For those reasons, the only guidelines you really have are to feed enough food to keep your bird happy and healthy, but not fat.

HOW OFTEN TO FEED?

Every bird needs to eat every day. Canaries, finches and other small birds will need to eat on and off throughout the day. Other birds will snack here and there, perhaps eating more in the morning or in the evening.

CHANGING YOUR BIRD'S FOOD

If you decide to change the food you are feeding your bird, don't do so abruptly. Many birds will refuse to eat when their food is changed, and others will suffer severe gastrointestinal upset, including diarrhea. Changes in the bird's diet must be made gradually.

If you are adding a commercial prepared food or are adding a new ingredient, make the change over a three-week period.

The first week, feed one-quarter of the new food and three-quarters of the old food. The second week, feed half the old food and half the new food. The third week, feed three-quarters of the new food and one-quarter of the old food. By the fourth week, the bird should be eating the new food with little or no gastrointestinal upset.

Changing a bird from seed to a pelleted food can take even longer with some birds. Soaking the pelleted food at first might help; the moist food is sometimes more appealing. However, some birds simply refuse to eat commercial pelleted foods.

THE IMPORTANCE OF CLEANLINESS

As a bird keeper, you must always be concerned with cleanliness. In the wild, your bird would not stay in one spot, day after day, sitting where its feces are. It would be flying from one spot to another, eating here, perching there, and maintaining a much larger territory than the small cage it lives in at your house.

Clean your bird's cage weekly, at a minimum—more often if needed. The cage can be wiped out with a diluted bleach solution and air dried. The bars of the cage should be washed each time you clean it and then scraped with a wire brush if droppings have hardened on them. Perches should be scraped and cleaned as needed.

Food and water dishes should be cleaned daily and disinfected with a diluted bleach solution, rinsed well and then allowed to air dry.

Keeping your bird's cage clean will help keep your bird healthy and will greatly decrease any objectionable odors that come from a dirty cage.

HAND FEEDING BABY BIRDS

Hand feeding baby birds is extremely rewarding but very time consuming. A hand-raised bird is quite different from one raised totally by its parents. The hand-raised bird is focused more on people instead of other birds and as a result, makes a wonderful pet. The birds most often hand fed include macaws, the various large and medium parrots, cockatoos and conures.

Some breeders allow the parents to incubate the eggs and feed their offspring for a few days to a week or so. This way the parents do much of the hard work of feeding the babies and keeping them warm. In the meantime, as they feed the babies, they are also passing on their immunities to their offspring. Then, when the babies are a week or two old, they can be pulled from their parents and hand fed until weaning.

Baby birds must be kept warm—about 80 to 90 degrees is good for most species for the first few weeks. After about six weeks of age, the babies can become accustomed to room temperature (about 72 degrees).

During the first week of life, baby birds need to eat every two hours around the clock. For weeks three through four, feeding times can be extended to every four hours between 6 a.m. and midnight. By week seven, most baby birds can be fed three times a day.

There are several hand feeding formulas on the market. Kaytee produces a food called Exact Original Hand Feeding Formula for all baby birds. The formula is mixed with water and a chart on the side of the food container tells how to mix the food, to what consistency and how much to feed. Other foods include similar directions.

When the baby birds are about six to seven weeks of age, put a bowl of pelleted bird food in the cage. The baby birds will explore these new things and eventually will taste and eat them. When the birds are eating the pelleted food, you can introduce other foods, including finely chopped vegetables, ground beans and sprouts. A bowl of water can be added now, too, shallow and small enough so that a young bird cannot accidentally drown.

HAVE I GOT IT RIGHT?

Because there are so few guidelines for proper feeding, you need to carefully watch your bird and adjust its diet according to how it responds, physically and psychologically, to its food. Here are some questions to ask yourself:

- Does your bird look healthy? Do the feathers look good or are they dull looking?
- Does the skin under the feathers look smooth and filled out, or is it bunchy, with unusual folds?
- Does there appear to be any problem with the skin on the bird's legs or feet, or on the ceres above the beak?
- Are your bird's eyes bright and alert?

- Is your bird at a good weight, neither too fat nor too thin? Is your bird eating all or most of its food?
- Is your bird's activity level normal or better than it used to be? Is it normal for your bird's species?
- Has there been any change in your bird's behavior that cannot be attributed to something in the environment?
- Are your bird's stools normal for its species? Has there been any change in the stools?
- Is the bird being used in a breeding program? If so, is it showing normal sex drive? Is it reproducing well? Are the eggs good and the offspring healthy?

If you can answer positively for all of these questions and your bird appears healthy, of good weight and is reproducing well (if that is one of your goals), then chances are you are feeding your bird properly.

TEN

FEEDING BACKYARD BIRDS

One-third of the United States adult population feeds wild birds in their backyard, according to Ralph M. Well of the National Bird-Feeding Society. "Providing food, water and shelter helps the birds survive, benefits the environment and supplements the birds' natural diet of weed seeds and insects."

I get a good feeling about feeding my neighborhood birds. I have five hummingbird feeders and several of those little jewels have staked out my backyard as their territory. I also have seed feeders and suet feeders that attract regular visitors.

I have learned to recognize certain individual birds and look for them each day. A female house finch has been raising two nests of babies each year for three years now in the cedar tree in my backyard. I know when she has a nest because she combs the yard for twigs, strings and even the hair I brush out of my dogs' winter coats. I hear the babies chirping once they've hatched, and when they do I start leaving out a pie pan with mealworms in it. She will hop down, take two or three mealworms, go feed her babies and come back for more. If I'm late with the mealworms, I will hear her scolding! Later, when she teaches her babies to fly, she will let them flutter around the backyard, even when I am there. I feel so trusted.

CREATING A BIRD SANCTUARY

FEEDING STATIONS. Once you decide to start feeding birds, it's important to offer food all year. Your feeder will probably never be the sole source of food for any bird; wild birds will still forage. However, the extra food you provide could easily mean the difference between good nutritional health and bad, or even the difference between life and death.

What type of food and feeders you put out depends upon the geographical area you live in and what type of bird you want to attract. Obviously, hummingbird feeders full of sugar water will attract hummingbirds only if they live in or migrate through your area. And hummingbird feeders won't attract any other type of bird, except perhaps orioles.

Hummingbird feeders come in a variety of sizes and shapes. As long as your local hummingbirds recognize the feeder as a source of food, it really doesn't matter what the feeder looks like. The same goes for oriole feeders. You can find feeders and nectar mixes at your local pet supply store, wild bird supply store or sometimes even the local discount store. Nectar and sugar water feeders should be cleaned weekly.

Seed feeders also come in a variety of sizes, shapes and styles. Some are designed to hang from the eaves of your house or from tree limbs. Others stand on top of a post. Choose a feeder style you like that is designed for the type of seed you are planning to put out.

Suet feeders are usually wire cages or net bags that will hold the suet and hang from the eaves of your house or the limbs of a tree. Suet should be replaced if it gets rancid.

Chart 15 shows some of the foods you can offer and the types of birds attracted to them.

CHART 15
WHAT WILD BIRDS LIKE TO EAT, BY SPECIES

Black Oil and Striped
  Sunflower Seeds
    Blue Jays
    Chickadees
    Doves
    Finches (House and Purple)
    Juncos
    Nuthatches
    Siskins
    Sparrows
    Titmice
    Woodpeckers

Millet
    Blackbirds
    Cardinals
    Cowbirds
    Doves
    Juncos
    Quail
    Sparrows
    Towhee
    Thrashers
    Thrushes

Baked Goods
(crumble up biscuits, stale bread, corn bread and other baked goods)
Bluebirds
Blue Jays
Flickers
Nuthatches
Orioles
Robins
Sparrows
Tanagers
Thrushes

Peanut Butter
Bluebirds
Chickadees
Mockingbirds
Orioles
Robins
Sparrows
Thrushes

Niger Seeds
Doves
Finches
Goldfinches
Juncos
Siskins
Sparrows

Safflower Seeds
Blue Jays
Chickadees
Finches
Nuthatches
Sparrows
Titmice

Fruit
(a variety of fruits sliced and diced, and berries such as currants)
Blue Jays
Cardinals
Catbirds
Finches
Grosbeaks
Mockingbirds
Orioles
Robins
Tanagers
Thrushes

Cracked Corn
Blackbirds
Blue Jays
Cardinals
Doves
Juncos
Quail
Sparrows
Starlings

Shelled Peanuts
Bluebirds
Cardinals
Cowbirds
Nuthatches
Sparrows
Woodpeckers

Suet
Chickadees
Flickers
Nuthatches
Titmice
Woodpeckers

KEEPING THE FEEDING STATIONS HEALTHY

If you find you are attracting quite a few birds, you may want to put up a few more feeders in different parts of your yard. When birds get too crowded, they are more likely to transmit diseases, especially as the birds start defecating in the food.

The feeders should also be cleaned at least once a week. Scrub the feeders with a diluted bleach solution and let them air dry.

If you find any dead birds that are obviously not the work of the neighborhood cat, call your local wildlife agency. Call, too, if you see any obviously sick birds.

Birds can be messy eaters and will toss seeds out of the feeder onto the ground. Eventually these seeds will sprout or will begin to decay. Rake up the mess weekly and dump it in your compost heap or trash.

LANDSCAPE FOR THE BIRDS

Many common landscape plants will offer backyard birds both shelter and, at certain times of the year, food. Chart 16 shows some of those plants and some of the birds attracted to them.

WATER IS LIFE

In many parts of the country you will be able to attract more birds with water than you will with food. In drier areas, or during the dry season, water is often hard to find. Unfortunately, too, much of the water wild birds do find is polluted. Most birds welcome clean water offered in a bird bath or even a large pie pan.

THE TOUCH OF NATURE

Backyard bird feeding is a wonderful way to touch nature. By providing foods for various birds, shelter from the elements, protection from predators and clean water, you can turn your backyard into a haven (or heaven on earth!) for birds.

CHART 16
THE LANDSCAPE PLANTS BIRDS LOVE

Wayfaring Bush, Nannyberry and Snowbush

- Bluebirds
- Blue Jays
- Cardinals
- Catbirds
- Flickers
- Grouse
- Mockingbirds
- Pheasants
- Robins
- Waxwings

Serviceberry, Chokecherry, Elderberry and Silky Dogwood

- Cardinals
- Catbirds
- Flickers
- Grosbeaks
- Kingbirds
- Mockingbirds
- Orioles
- Robins
- Sparrows
- Tanagers
- Thrashers
- Thrushes
- Vireos
- Waxwings
- Woodpeckers

CHART 17
NUTRITIONAL COMPARISONS OF WILD BIRD FOODS

While this is by no means a complete list of all the wild bird foods available, it will give you an idea of the ingredients in wild bird foods and how to compare them.

SEEDS AND SEED MIXTURES

Kaytee Sunflower Seeds

Protein	16.5%
Fat	25%
Fiber	29%
Moisture	12%

Ingredients: oil sunflower seed

CHART 17, CONTINUED,
NUTRITIONAL COMPARISONS OF
WILD BIRD FOOD

Kaytee Garden Valley
Wild Bird Food

Protein	10.2%
Fat	4.1%
Fiber	14.3%
Moisture	9.1%

Ingredients: milo, white millet, red millet, wheat, oil sunflower seed

HUMMINGBIRD AND ORIOLE NECTARS

Perky Pet Brand Instant
Nectar for Hummingbirds

Protein	.01%
Fat	.01%
Fiber	.1%
Total sugars as invert:	100%

Ingredients: sucrose, dextrose, tartaric acid, sodium benzoate (preservative), artificial coloring and flavoring

SEED TREATS, BALLS OR BELLS

Wild Bird Black Oil
Sunflower Seed Bell

Protein	15%
Fat	28%
Fiber	25%
Moisture	12%

Ingredients: black oil sunflower seed, gelatin

Kaytee Honey Mixed
Seed Treat

Protein	10%
Fat	4%
Fiber	10%
Moisture	14%

Ingredients: white millet, sunflower, red millet, milo, gelatin, honey, dextrose

SUET FOODS AND TREATS

C & S Products Peanut Delight Suet Dough

Protein 10%
Fat 20%
Fiber 4%

Ingredients: rendered beef suet, peanuts, corn, oats (attracts suet- and nut-eating birds, including woodpeckers, chickadees and nuthatches)

C & S Products Berry Treat

Protein 4%
Fat 25%
Fiber 12%

Ingredients: rendered beef suet, millet, berry flavoring, corn (attracts fruit-eating birds, including orioles)

Wild Birds Unlimited Fruit Cakes Suet Dough with Fruit

Protein 6%
Fat 15%
Fiber 5%

Ingredients: rendered beef suet, peanuts, papaya, orange flavoring, corn, oats (attracts fruit-eating birds, including orioles)

Wild Birds Unlimited Bird Bug Bites Suet Dough with Insects

Protein 5%
Fat 15%
Fiber 5%

Ingredients: rendered beef suet, dehydrated insects, corn (attracts any suet- and insect-eating birds, including woodpeckers, chickadees, nuthatches, finches and wrens)

Wild Birds Unlimited Cravin' Raisin Suet Dough with Raisins

Protein 5%
Fat 14%
Fiber 5%

Ingredients: rendered beef suet, raisins, corn, oats (attracts suet-eating birds, including woodpeckers, chickadees and nuthatches, and also attracts fruit-eating birds, including orioles)

Wild Birds Unlimited Almond Munch Suet Dough with Almonds

Protein 12%
Fat 20%
Fiber 4%

Ingredients: rendered beef suet, roasted almonds, corn, oats (attracts suet- and nut-eating birds, including woodpeckers, chickadees and nuthatches)

APPENDIX 1

BIRD FOOD SUPPLIERS AND MANUFACTURERS

SEEDS, SEED MIXTURES AND COMMERCIAL FOODS

8 in 1 Pet Products
Hauppauge, NY 11788

AlphaPet Inc.
4914 Daggett
St. Louis, MO 63110

Amazon Smythe Trading Corporation
(800) 529-8331

American Bird Products
(703) 536-2473 or (540) 854-5562

C & S Products, Inc.
Fort Dodge, IA 50501

Fanta Seeds
Halo, 3438 East Lake Road #14
Palm Harbor, FL 34685

Hagen Avicultural Research Institute
Rolf C. Hagen Corporation, PO Box 9107
Manfield, MA 02048
(800) 225-2700

Hartz Mountain Corp.
Secaucus, NJ 07094

Kaylor-Made Products
1015 E. Cotati Ave.
Cotati, CA 94931-0024
(800) 535-5399

Kaytee Avian Research Center
(800) KAYTEE-1

L'Avian Plus
D & D Commodities Ltd.
Highway 75 South, PO Box 359
Stephen, MN 56757
(800) 543-3308

Lafeber Company
24981 N. 1400 East Road,
Cornell, IL 61319
(800) 842-6445 x163

LM Animal Farms
Pleasant Plain, OH 45162
(800) 332-5623

Lyng's Sunflower Seeds
Trinidad/Benham Corp.
1868 Clayton Road, #223
Concord, CA 94520
(510) 689-5511

Marion Zoological Inc.
13803 Industrial Park Blvd.
Plymouth, MN 55441
(800) 327-7974

Mauro's Inc.
756 Perry Taylor Road
Leesville, SC 29070

Noah's Kingdom
326 Broad St.
Red Bank, NJ 07701
(800) 662-4711

Nutriphase, distributed by Pacific Coast Distributing
PO Box 84613
Phoenix AZ 85701-4613

Perky Pet Products, Inc.
2201 S. Wabash St.
Denver, CO 80231

Pretty Bird International, Inc.
5810 Stacy Trail
Stacy, MN 55079
(800) 356-5020

Rowdybush
1166 Broadway #L
Placerville, CA 94556
(800) 326-1726

Sun Seeds
PO Box 33
Bowling Green, OH 43402
(800) 221-6175

Sunshine Bird Supplies
8535 NW 56 St.
Miami, FL 33166
(800) 878-2666

HAND REARING BABY BIRD FORMULAS

Kellogg Inc.
Milwaukee, WI 53201

LM Animal Farms
Neo-Nate
Pleasant Plain, OH 45162
(800) 332-5623

Marion Zoological Inc.
13803 Industrial Park Blvd.
Plymouth, MN 55441
(800) 327-7974

Pretty Bird
5810 Stacy Trail
Stacy, MN 55079
(800) 356-5020

TOYS, TREATS, VITAMINS AND SUPPLEMENTS

8 in 1 Pet Products
Hauppauge, NY 11788

Bir-Dee (food, treat bricks)
215 S. Averill
Flint, MI 48506
(800) 355-5517

Bird Yum (pasta, miscellaneous foods and treats)
7621 Fulton Ave.
N. Hollywood, CA 91605
(800) 247-3986

Cuttlebone Plus (lory nectar, spray millet and more)
PO Box 305
Fallbrook, CA 92088
(800) 747-9878

Garden Goodies
Sun Seeds
PO Box 33
Bowling Green, OH 43402
(800) 221-6175

Jungle Talk International
PO Box 111
Lafayette, CO 80026
(800) 247-3869

Kong Toys
11111D W. 8th Ave.
Lakewood, CO 80215
(309) 233-9262

Lambert Kay; Carter Wallace, Inc.
Cranbury, NJ 08512-0187

Mardel Laboratories, Inc.
Glendale Heights, IL 60139

Oasis; Novalek, Inc.
2242 Davis Court
Hayward, CA 94545

Scooter's Pet Products
4200 Park Blvd. #116
Oakland, CA 94602
(415) 206-2003

INSECT SUPPLIERS

Arbico
PO Box 4247
Tucson, AZ 85738-1247
(800) 827-2847

Rainbow Mealworms
126 E. Spruce St., PO Box 4907
Compton, CA 90224
(800) 777-9676

BIRD SUPPLIES, INCLUDING FEEDING BOWLS AND WATERERS

Bird Buddy (miscellaneous supplies)
733 Kris Lane
Mosinee, WI 54455
(715) 693-6471

Bird Country Aviary Bedding
Mountain Meadows Pet, PO Box 778
Lewistown, MT 59457
(800) 752-8864

Duro Test (full spectrum lights)
Vita Lite Plus
(800) 688-5826

JV Products (bowls)
(800) 848-3064

Lixit (water bottles)
PO Box 876
Newport Richey, FL 34656
(707) 252-1622

Oasis (water bottles)
Novalek, 2242 Davis Court
Hayward, CA 94545-1114
(800) 877-7387

Pennington Pet Products (cuttlebone holder)
Rt. 1, Box 3731B
Mountain City, TN 37683

That Pet Place (miscellaneous supplies)
237 Centerville Road
Lancaster, PA 17603
(717) 299-5691

APPENDIX 2

FOR MORE INFORMATION

MAGAZINES

Here are the major aviculture magazines, along with where to write for a subscription and how much they cost.

Bird Breeder
PO Box 420246
Palm Coast, FL 32142-9481
$29.97 per year/12 issues

Bird Talk
PO Box 57347
Boulder, CO 80323-7347
$26.97 per year/12 issues

Birder's World
PO Box 1612
Waukesha, WI 53187-9950
$14.95 per year/6 issues

Birds USA Annual
Fancy Publications
PO Box 6050
Mission Viejo, CA 92690

Caged Bird Hobbyist
7-L Dundas Circle
Greensboro, NC 27407
$19.25 per year/6 issues

Living Bird
Cornell Lab of Ornithology
PO Box 11
Ithaca, NY 14851-9803
free to members (membership is $35 a year)

Wild Bird
PO Box 52898
Boulder, CO 80322-2898
$23.97 per year/12 issues

CLUBS AND SOCIETIES

African Lovebird Society
PO Box 142
San Marcos, CA 92069

African Parrot Society
PO Box 204-CB
Clarinda, IA 51632-2731

American Budgerigar Society
1704 Kangaroo
Killeen, TX 76543

American Canary Fanciers
13687 Camilla
Whittier, CA 90601

American Cockatiel Society
9527 60th Lane N.
Pinellas Park, FL 34666
        or
PO Box 609
Fruitland Park, FL 34731

American Federation of Aviculture
PO Box 56218
Phoenix, AZ 85079

Aviculture Society of America
PO Box 5516
Riverside, CA 92517

Bird Clubs of America
PO Box 2005
Yorktown, VA 23692

International Aviculturists Society (IAS)
14415 Dabney Court
Spring Hill, FL 34610

National Parrot Association
8 N. Hoffman Lane
Hauppauge, NY 11788

Pionus Breeders Association
1106 Roswell
Pomona, CA 91766

Society of Parrot Breeders and Exhibitors
PO Box 369
Groton, MA 01450

BIBLIOGRAPHY

Abramson, Joanne. "The Beautiful Macaws," *Birds USA Annual*, 1995/1996, pp. 32–35.

Allen, Gloria. "The Joys of Owning a Cockatoo," *Birds USA Annual*, 1995/1996, pp. 46–48.

American Association of Feed Control Officials. Georgia Department of Agriculture, Atlanta, GA, (404) 656-3637.

Anderson, Jean, MS and Barbara Deskins, PhD, RD. *The Nutrition Bible*. New York: William Morrow and Co., 1995.

Brancato, Tony. "Pigeons and Doves," *Birds USA Annual*, 1995/1996, pp. 50–57.

Chamberlain, Susan. "Engaging Psittacula Parakeets," *Birds USA Annual*, 1995/1996, pp. 82–84.

Christian, Michael S. "The Budgerigar: More Than a Childhood Memory," *Birds USA Annual*, 1995/1996, pp. 36–38.

Desborough, Laurella. "Enchanting Eclectus," *Birds USA Annual*, 1995/1996, pp. 118–120.

Dorge, Raymond. "Falling for Lovebirds," *Birds USA Annual*, 1995/1996, pp. 58–60.

Dorge, Raymond. "Increasing Lovebird Clutches," *Bird Breeder,* Vol. 67, No. 5, May 1995, pp. 40–45.

Dunne, Lavon J. *Nutrition Almanac,* Third Ed. New York: McGraw-Hill Publishing Co., 1990.

Eddy, Brian. "Breeding the Yellow-Shouldered Amazon," *Bird Breeder,* Vol. 67, No. 5, May 1995, pp. 26–29.

Gerstenfekd, Sheldon L., VDM. *The Bird Care Book.* Reading, MA: Addison-Wesley Publishing Co., 1989.

Grindol, Diane. "Charming Cockatiels," *Birds USA Annual,* 1995/1996, pp. 78–81.

Haas, Elson M., M.D. *Staying Healthy With Nutrition.* Berkeley, CA: Celestial Arts, 1992.

Harris, Robbie. "Beloved Brotogeris," *Birds USA Annual,* 1995/1996, pp. 122–126.

Harris, Robbie. "The Wonder of Poicephalus Parrots," *Birds USA Annual,* 1995/1996, pp. 112–117.

Hinke, Ian. "Finches: The Ideal Choice," *Birds USA Annual,* 1995/1996, pp. 86–89.

Howse, Susan and Gayle Anderson Nixon. "Those Magnetic Mynahs," *Caged Bird Hobbyist,* Vol. 4, No. 1, Jan./Feb. 1996, pp. 27, 51.

McWatters, Alicia. "Preventive Care of the Avian Digestive System," *Bird Breeder,* Vol. 67, No. 5, May 1995, pp. 58–59.

Paradise, Paul A. *African Grey Parrots.* Neptune City, NJ: TFH Publications, 1979.

Perea, Ignacio, Sr. "Taking Note of the Canary," *Birds USA Annual,* 1995/1996, p. 44.

Pet Food Institute and Nutrition Assurance Program. 1200 19th St. NW, Suite 300, Washington, D.C. 20036, (800) 851-0769.

Pitcairn, Richard H. and Susan Hubble Pitcairn. *Dr. Pitcairn's Guide to Natural Health for Dogs and Cats*. Emmaus, PA: Rodale Press, 1982.

Plechner, Alfred J. and Martin Zucker. *Pet Allergies: Remedies for an Epidemic*. Inglewood, CA: Very Healthy Enterprises, 1986.

Samuelson, Kathleen. "Bird's Eye View: Basic Instincts," *Bird Talk*, Vol. 14, No. 5, May 1996, p. 4.

Sefton, David. "Lories and Lorikeets," *Birds USA Annual*, 1995/1996. pp. 94–97.

Silva, Tony. "Dietary Supplements for Healthier Birds," *The Pet Dealer*, Vol. 43, No. 7, July 1994, pp. 48–51.

Soderberg, P.M. *All About Lovebirds*. Neptune City, NJ: TFH Publications, 1977.

Teitler, Risa. *Taming and Training Cockatoos*. Neptune City, NJ: TFH Publications, 1980.

Vriends, Mathew M., PhD. *The New Bird Handbook*. Hauppauge, NY: Barron's Educational Series, 1989.

Vriends, Mathew M., PhD. *The New Cockatiel Handbook*. Hauppauge, NY: Barron's Educational Series, 1989.

Well, Ralph M. "Other Views: One-Third of Americans Feed Backyard Songbirds," *Caged Bird Hobbyist*, Vol. 4, No. 1, Jan./Feb. 1996, p. 17.

Wild Birds Unlimited. *Seed Preference Guide* and *Berry Bushes and the Birds They Attract*. 2624-F El Camino Real, Carlsbad, CA 92008.

Wilson, Liz. "Avian Behavior: The Psychological Dangers of Weaning," *Caged Bird Hobbyist*, Vol. 4, No. 1, Jan./Feb. 1996, pp. 10, 50.

Wissman, Margaret, DVM. "A Conure for All Seasons," *Birds USA Annual*, 1995/1996, pp. 28–30.

Witty, Helen and Dick Witty. *Feed the Birds*. New York: Workman Publishing, 1991.

INDEX

127